GARDENDESIGNERS
AT HOME

GARDENDESIGNERS
AT HOME

The Private Spaces of the World's Leading Designers

Noel Kingsbury

PAVILION

Contents

Introduction

What do garden designers do at home? It is always interesting to
know what the members of any profession do when they do not
have to earn money or please a client. There are, of course, examples
of the proverbial cobbler's unshod children – Lanning Roper, one of the
most highly regarded British designers of the 1950s and 1960s, notoriously
never had a garden, merely a yard where plants were stored en route to clients'
gardens. The vast majority of garden designers, however, do garden, sometimes
publicly, so that their gardens are an important part of their presentation
of their work, others privately – their gardens being purely for private or
family satisfaction.

As background to our look at what garden designers get up to "behind the scenes",
it is worth taking a closer look at who garden designers are and what they do. Firstly,
we need to understand that the profession of "garden designer" is not one that is
universally recognised. In many countries, the work of designing private gardens
is nearly always carried out by those who regard themselves as "landscape designers"
or "landscape architects", for whom the private commission is worked on alongside
those done for public clients: corporations, municipalities, institutions. Britain is
unusual in that its historic pattern of human settlement has resulted in a large
proportion of the population having private gardens. This, and a climate friendly
to mixing and matching plants from varied regions, has resulted in a kind of
horticultural heaven. Here is one of the very few places where a large number of
successful careers have been built as garden designers. The Netherlands is another
rare example where the separate profession of garden designer is recognized.

In any country, the training of landscape (as opposed to garden) designers is very
largely about learning the skills of working with spatial relationships and how to
physically bring about the changes in these relationships. So landscape professionals
are primarily concerned with grades, perspectives, volumes of space, surface
materials and constructional details. Plant selection and plant management is simply
another module on the course, and one that does not concern most landscape
professionals very deeply. In many countries, there are additional reasons why
planting design has a low priority – historically, landscape design has often
originated as an offshoot of architecture, and architects nearly always have
a higher status than those who work the land: farmers, gardeners or foresters.
In those places (most notably Britain) where there is enough work to support a
profession dedicated to garden making alone, the professional map is different –
many garden designers are first and foremost horticulturalists. With the selection of
appropriate plants for a site their priority, and an extensive knowledge of how those
plants will develop over time with different techniques, the horticulture-orientated
designer is interested in developing a dynamic relationship between space and plant.
However, those who are basically landscape professionals all too often tend to see
plants only as static filler material.

In selecting the designers to feature in this book, there has been a strong bias towards designers who, whatever their professional background, are known for their skill in using plants. It is my belief that plants are absolutely central to the whole concept of a garden, and that good planting design skills are integral to good garden design. Here it is perhaps worth stressing my own professional interest, and in so doing admit to my opinions and biases – and say a little about my own garden.

I work primarily as a writer and teacher, concerned with horticulture, planting design, ecology and, to a lesser extent, food. My professional design work is only concerned with planting; I am occasionally asked to design someone's garden, which I very much enjoy, although what I really find most stimulating is working as part of a team, where I create interesting plantings in the context of others' work with the "hard" elements of the landscape. I also very much enjoy creating high-visibility plantings for public places, such as roundabouts and traffic islands; part of this is the challenge of bringing natural beauty to gritty urban surroundings.

A BORDER of perennials in the author's garden (previous page) – as are all the pictures in this introduction. The tall pink is a wild collection of *Eupatorium fistulosum* from North Carolina. Beyond the border is a wildflower meadow – home to a yurt for summer guests.

A WILD garden area on very wet soil with *Sanguisorba caucasica* in front (above). Very robust species are chosen for this area and these will co-exist with minimal maintenance – which is limited to occasional weeding and an annual cut-back.

Much of my work has been concerned with applying the questions raised by plant ecology to garden situations – why does this plant thrive here, why is this combination a stable one, what will happen if this plant is allowed to self-sow its seeds here? My own garden, which I share with my partner Jo, is very largely a series of ongoing, and hopefully beautiful, experiments. Some of these are experiments in a formal sense of the word – I've recently completed a research doctorate with the Landscape Department of Sheffield University and continue to be an Associate there. Others are more loosely geared to trialling either new plants, or novel management techniques. The largest feature in the garden is a herbaceous border, 20m (65ft) long, up to 5m (16ft) wide, where a variety of plants are intermingled, but all are planted in lines, 1m (3ft) apart. For most of the year, the lines are completely invisible, but they do allow for annual monitoring, so that I can record the position of everything on the line in a database, which functions also as a topological plan of the border.

Conventional planting design is static – plants are placed according to the designer's specification, and they are expected to stay there. Natural plant communities are, however, dynamic, so that individuals are always regenerating (through seeds, or suckers or adventurous shoots) or dying. I am

TEST-BEDS for research purposes and stock-beds for the production of plants for jobs are part of a functional 'nursery' area. Late summer sees a profusion of flower – much of it yellow or violet-blue, a colour mix which is very common in North America, from where many of our border perennials originate.

interested in the extent to which this can happen without being too disruptive to the conception of the planting as an aesthetic creation. Management is crucial to how this kind of planting develops, as it is with any garden. The extent to which garden designers are involved with the ongoing supervision of their plantings varies enormously; needless to say, it is the more horticulturally orientated amongst them who make return visits, supervise staff, and advise on changes.

What I do in my garden is not necessarily what I would do in a client's. And this is true of nearly all the designers I spoke to during the course of researching this book. Time and time again I was told that "Here I can do what I want to do." Because gardens are living entities, subject to constant change, any garden is in fact an experiment. As designers we wish our experiments to be successful, but there is always a risk. We minimize this risk for a garden or planting over which we know we will have little further influence, increase it for an understanding client with whom we have an ongoing relationship, and increase it further for ourselves. Nearly every designer takes more risks with their own garden, and they regard that risk as being part of the fun – in particular, the opportunity to grow favoured, but unpredictable plants. Experimenting and risk taking, particularly with new plants, is also part of the ongoing process of "R&D" (research and development) in which most garden designers are actively engaged – what works in their garden today, may be found in clients' tomorrow.

Fundamentally though, garden designers' gardens are personal spaces, just as anyone's garden is a personal space. Some designers may use their gardens to entertain clients, to show what they can do, but most tend to see the garden in the opposite light, as somewhere to practise their art for their personal benefit. I do, however, have a sneaking suspicion that certain designers don't like actual gardening – part of me would have liked to include photographs of their hands in this book, so that we could see who had dirty fingernails or callouses from holding a spade rather than a pen. For many, though, the sheer physicality of gardening is clearly something they enjoy, and their own gardens are a place to experience this to the full.

Favourite Plants

Every designer has been asked for some of his or her favourite or signature plants. Needless to say, these are very much "of the moment", as in many cases I am sure that they would list different plants if I asked them a week later! That said, these plant suggestions are a useful guide to species that do not just look good, but which perform reliably enough to be used over and over again in clients' gardens.

The United States Department of Agriculture Hardiness Zones are given wherever possible. These are a very useful guide to the minimum temperatures a plant will grow at over most of the continental USA and Canada, less so for the North American west coast and certainly less so for Europe. The temperature ranges represented by USDA zones are given in many garden reference books or online.

James Alexander-Sinclair Blackpitts, Northamptonshire, UK

"I LOVE THIS GARDEN, every day is a delight, but it's weird, as it is so inward looking," says James. "It is frustrating because it has no wider landscape and no west aspect… and working with transitions to the wider landscape is what I really like doing. This is the garden I have stayed in the longest, but we won't be here for more than five years. I want the challenge of starting again, I've got one more big project in me."

The surroundings here are disused agricultural buildings, constructed in traditional red brick, so James feels that including some industrial materials, such as steel flooring or tubing, is appropriate, not just for its value in adding a contemporary touch. Even so, hard elements play a pretty minor role – this garden is firmly about plants. It is full of vibrant colour: orange poppies, scarlet sanguisorbas, drifts of violet *Verbena bonariensis*, magenta *Geranium psilostemon*, but none of it is on top of anything else, as there is plenty of green and plenty of structure. It is clearly the garden of someone who loves plants and is not afraid of engaging in some time-consuming, and very traditional, horticultural skills – the north wall of the house is home to two very large and meticulously pruned and trained espalier pyracanthas. "This garden is intense, its

THE VIEW from an upper storey of the house. Beech columns inject a sense of order, just in case the perennials get too out of hand. The silver tree in the corner of the old farm buildings is Coyote willow (*Salix exigua*) – a delicate-looking but robust small tree.

BIOGRAPHY "I had very little further education" recalls James (born 1959), "but gardening, education and sex – they are three things that are lost on the young... I'd been a photographer and a gossip columnist for a magazine called *Monocle* and then for the *Daily Express*, before doing a ten week garden design course at the Inchbald in 1984", and then "stumbling into being a garden construction contractor, the last resort of the unemployable." He built a successful career designing and building gardens, but when he and his wife Celestria moved to Blackpitts in 1992, he dropped the physical side of the work and concentrated purely on design.

James's career has included some presenting on television gardening programmes, a garden at the Chelsea Flower Show (1999) and the Westonbirt Garden Festival (2004). Most of his work has been for private clients, and he prefers to work on large country gardens, where he can build up a relationship with the owner over many years. He may say, "the clients are not entitled to their own opinions", but then admits that sitting around chatting and discussing the garden is a big part of the job.

James's style is primarily focused on planting, although his background as a contractor gives him plenty of confidence in working with hard features. "Plants used to come second," he says, "but now they come first... small gardens in the city are different, you have to make them like the outside room, which John Brookes talks about, but in the countryside you want a garden, with plants and, I think, you need to bleed the garden into the landscape so you cannot tell where the join is."

Renowned for his imaginative prose, James's blog (web. mac.com/blackpittsgarden) has become much-read for its witty and trenchantly expressed opinions – "Garden design is, I would imagine, a bit like having a brief but extraordinarily energetic affair with somebody else's wife. There comes a moment when you have to walk away with a whisper of regret and a lingering scent in your nostrils." He is not afraid to voice opinions that others would rather keep quiet about – the huge increase in numbers in the profession during the 1990s and 2000s leads him to comment that "garden designers are like handbags – people are now realizing that they don't need so many."

GARDENS OPEN TO THE PUBLIC

- **Mount Stuart** Isle of Bute, Argyll and Bute, Scotland – the kitchen garden and areas around the visitor centre.

- **Cottesbrooke Hall** Northamptonshire. Several borders.

one big border is crammed with plants," he says. "The secret is to have enough to hide the weeds... my style is to use lots of plants, not the clean urban look; the more plants you use, then the more potential combinations there are." Visiting in mid-winter on a desperately dull day, it is still full of interest: blonde grass seed head stems reach skywards, and there are clumps of deepest brown perennial foliage and enough evergreen foliage to give some relief from the yellow to brown spectrum.

"The delight of one's own garden is that there ain't no client, you don't have to take anyone's feelings into consideration, although you have to deal with one's wife and children," says James. Experimentation is a big part of his gardening and, since one of his greatest joys is finding a nursery selling plants he has not seen before,

this is clearly an important function. "We are on heavy clay in the middle of the country," he states, "so if it grows well here it will do well in most other places."

Experimentation is about aesthetics too, he explains: "I didn't do orange until I came here. Working here has given me confidence in my ability with colour... advanced level planting design involves serious colour... I am way beyond all those Rosemary Verey loo-paper colours, easy because you can't go wrong with them." The number of self-sowing annuals and perennials in the garden indicates an embrace, maybe even a love, of the role of the ephemeral and the temporary. "I consciously use trial and error," he says. "You just play with stuff; after all, plants are not fluffy kittens, you can dig them up and compost them if they don't work or you get bored

with them." Getting bored with plants is something that is mentioned several times, and when asked for his "top six" he says they will probably be different tomorrow. The constant (literal) chopping and changing with the yew hedge along one side of the garden is another example of this love of novelty – not many people would be so experimental with a hedge, or so happy with one that is so irregular.

In creating a garden surrounded by traditional farm buildings on all four sides, many people would design traditionally, echoing the straight lines of the architecture with axes and alleys. James's garden eschews these clichés, so it comes across as completely, but gently, contemporary. The atmosphere is of someone having fun, who is passionate about plants and takes risks, a place with an uninhibited quality.

ANNUAL opium poppies (*Papaver somniferum*) consort with a variety of perennials and bulbs (*above*); the prominent flowerhead in the lower-left is *Allium christophii*.

"It's not an artwork, but an unfinished pond" says James of the steel structure (*right*).

TIMELINE

1995–6 Initially the garden was a concrete farmyard, with no soil. The concrete was removed, topsoil was trucked in and it was grassed over. A wooden pergola was built at one end.

1998 The parterre, with slate paths, was constructed.

2001 Beech trees were planted in a geometrical arrangement in the lawn, which have since been cut into square columns. "The yews give a good framing effect, and the grass was nice for the children to run around on." The yews were from the 1999 Chelsea garden planted out to form a free-form and sculptural hedge along one side, "which I change in shape every year," says James.

2002 The wooden pergola fell down, so it was replaced with steel tubing.

2003 Built the 'grass snake' – a winding mound with a path running along the top – with left-over topsoil; from which the rest of the garden can be seen from a height, James reported that "one side of it was planted with festuca grasses, but they didn't work so we used *Anemanthele lessoniana* instead."

2007 Decking and steps were built to replace a grass slope, which led from the house to the lawn "as someone fell down it and broke their ankle," James recalls.

THE WINTER foliage of beech is echoed by leaving dead perennials and grasses for as long as possible. Grasses stand the wet and windy winters of Britain better than flowering perennials on the whole.

17

Some Favourite Plants

Persicaria polymorpha (Aconogonon 'Johanniswolke')

As James explains, "It sits there in flower for ever, it keeps on giving the love." An enormous perennial, with the bulk of a shrub (2 x 2m/6½ x 6½ft), this relative of the Japanese knotweed does not run, making it immensely useful for creating seasonal mass. Cream flowers from June on, fading to pink. Fertile soil and good levels of soil moisture are needed. Sun or light shade.
ZONE 3 MIN.

Rosa laevigata 'Cooper's Burmese'

A climbing rose that James loves for its red stems and bronzy glossy foliage – it really is one of the best roses for foliage. Cream flowers and dull orange hips. If given a sheltered position, it will grow to 5 x 5m (16 x 16ft), although it is probably not hardy in continental climates.
ZONE 6 MIN.

Fagus sylvatica beech

James likes to use beech as topiary and says: "I love it as a tree, it knocks the socks off an oak." Easy to grow on all well-drained soils, beech is particularly successful on thin calcareous ones and a notably good windbreak. The habit of clipped plants keeping their dead leaves over the winter makes it a useful plant for this season. Clear yellow autumn colour.
ZONE 4 MIN.

Papaver somniferum opium poppy

Salix exigua coyote willow

Dianthus carthusianorum

"I couldn't live without this poppy – it's haphazard, ephemeral, with nice seed heads so it dies slowly", says James. An annual growing to around 1-m (3ft) high, the big floppy flowers in shades of pink, cream, mauve and lilac are short-lived, but followed by fat seed pods that stand for much of the winter, scattering seed for next year's crop.

As James notes, "it gives a lot of height, I use it like a bamboo, for verticality and transparency." Its elongated silver leaves give it great garden potential. It eventually becomes a tree up to 3m (10ft) high, with a spread of 4m (13ft). Like bamboo it spreads by suckers that need to be removed if a thicket is to be avoided. Any soil is suitable if it is not too dry, and it is very successful on wet soil. ZONE 4 MIN.

The intensity of the magenta-pink makes up for the diminutive size of the flowers of this pink. So does its long summer flowering season, and its ability to flourish and flower in very dry conditions. Its 60cm (2ft) stems may seem gawky, but they are perfect for threading through grasses and other perennials of a similar size. Full sun. Alkaline soil preferred. ZONE 4 MIN.

Isabel and Julian Bannerman Hanham Court, Bristol, UK

ISABEL AND Julian Bannerman's own garden occupies an unusual site of great historic interest – a monastery once occupied it. Midway between the cities of Bath and Bristol in southwest England, it is an island of tranquillity in what has become a distinctly suburbanised landscape. The village church is still attached to the house, while a venerable tithe barn[1] stands to one side. The garden, on the south side of the house takes up about 0.8 hectares (2 acres), divided between a formal area and a dell – a wilder, wooded area. The formal garden occupies a bastion extending out from the house, supported on two sides by medieval walls – it is a bit like being on a ship as you stand well above the surroundings. "The location reminds me of Italian gardens," says Isabel, "which meant it had to be formal… we have created boxes to put different things in."

Isabel records that "It was Julian who fell in love with it at first, the downland and dell, so much up and down in a small area, a mini-world, acid on one side, alkaline on the other." The alkaline side of the garden is actually a surviving scrap of the limestone downland, once a major feature of landscapes around Bristol and Bath. It is rich in wild flowers, and home to a young orchard of heritage apple varieties, and provides a good

A HISTORICAL SITE such as this is often best reflected in some way in the planting. Clipping of trees (these are yew) was particularly popular in the 17th century. The profusion of perennials is much more 20th century.

BIOGRAPHY Isabel (born 1962) and Julian (1951) have spent most of their lives designing gardens together – since 1987 – after meeting in Edinburgh, where Isabel read history at the university and Julian was working in the contemporary art world and running a bar (of somewhat Bohemian repute; full of tramps and poets, Isabel hastens to add). Julian's work involved close association with many of the leading figures of the 1970s: he worked for Richard Demarco (1930–) a cultural entrepreneur and key figure in establishing the Edinburgh Fringe Festival, and introduced artists such as Joseph Beuys (1921–86), who was "incredibly influential", and James Turrell (1943–) to the British art world. Ian Hamilton Finlay (1925–2006), whose garden of text and poetry, south of Edinburgh, has been one of the most noticed by those outside the world of gardening, was a friend and exhibited regularly at the gallery. "What Demarco, and all these others emphasised," explains Julian, "is the importance of the artist working outside the studio walls."

"Julian has always loved gardening, and we both got gripped, longed to do things for other people and were in need of work when we were asked to design a garden building, using a collection of fossils and crystals belonging to Candida Lycett-Green... It was our break that lead to work for the Rothschilds at Waddesdon, restoring the dairy rock garden and then designing the award-winning dairy building itself... that was our first really big job," explains Isabel.

Isabel and Julian have gone on from one prestigious job to another, developing a style that is absolutely unique. Clients have included The Prince of Wales at Highgrove, Sir John Paul Getty, Andrew Lloyd Webber and, most recently, The British Memorial Garden Trust for a garden at Ground Zero in New York.

Back in the 1980s and early 1990s, garden design in Britain was in danger of becoming obsessed by a po-faced preoccupation with "period" and "traditional" design. The Bannermans took all of that, thrust it into a food processor and had fun. They make a pastiche of every European historical style and then pastiche that. It is rampantly, exuberantly, sumptuously over-the-top über-Romanticism. The Italian Renaissance, the Baroque, the Rococo, classicism, the mock-Gothic and the Gothick Revival – all are plundered, melted down and reworked into a seething and voluptuous confectionary of pyramids, columns, obelisks, faux tufa, grottoes, topiary, fountains and pleaching.

Whilst it is the structures that seize the attention in a Bannerman-designed garden – indeed, they have often been asked to design stand-alone garden architecture – the couple are also consummate planting designers, favouring a romantic English style, using topiary, roses and scented flowers. As they say, "We like green gardens and indigenous planting, understatement is what we are really about."

GARDENS OPEN TO THE PUBLIC

- **Hanham court** (the designers' own garden), Bristol.

- **The Collector Earl's Garden** Arundel Castle, Sussex.

- **Ashall Manor**, Oxfordshire.

- **Houghton Hall**, Norfolk.

- **The Dairy at Waddesdon**, Buckinghamshire.

vantage point from which to admire the garden. As the ground drops away on the western side of the garden to form a small valley, the soil becomes more acidic – this has been made into an informal area with a central pool and woodland planting.

Formality is what the Bannermans are renowned for, and so it is no surprise that the upper part of the garden is dominated by features that lay out a decisive structure – regularly repeated yew "flasks" and straight paths defined by neatly clipped box. In spring, tulips bring exuberant colours to the borders, while summer belongs to the roses – mostly old-fashioned varieties and a range of herbaceous plants. The paths and the view strongly direct you to walk towards the "bows" of the garden, on the way encountering a paved area with a small swimming pool. This is backed by a grotto, with an accompanying façade of architectural salvage and stone; the atmosphere is sheltered enough

1 A type of barn used to store grain delivered to the Church as part of taxation in pre-Reformation Britain.

ARROW CONES of yew
and mounds of box
seem almost to have
personalities. One great
advantage of them is their
long season of interest and
continuity, to say nothing of
their sense of antiquity.

here for the realisation of what Isabel and Julian regard as one of the most important aspects of gardening – scent.

"My first passion is scent," says Isabel. "If a plant doesn't have it, it's not very high on my list." There is no doubt that scent is a hugely underrated aspect of garden design; owing to the fact that its appreciation is dependent upon still air, design is a major factor in making the most of this most evanescent quality. Isabel points out that what they call the swimming pool garden, which has a wall protecting it from the prevailing wind, "traps scent" – so that the roses and honeysuckle, and lilies and heliotrope in pots can be appreciated to the full.

The garden at Hanham Court is actually a lot more sedate than much of their commissioned work. "We couldn't possibly afford the

architectural fantasia we provide for clients," says Isabel. She also agrees when I say that clients can have too much choice… whereas we are always having to "make-do" and sometimes that is more constructive, although sometimes it is just frustrating. Making this garden also sounds like it has been something of a physical challenge too. "The whole upper garden", explained Isabel, "is very free-draining and rocky, some areas are very dry… we think there were buildings here originally, part of the monastery… when we came there were shrubs and trees all around, sycamore and *leylandii*, blocking out the view."

One area that represents the Bannerman's characteristic design of structures is just south of the church. Here, there is a formal layout, dominated by oak seats, with head-high obelisk finials making a powerful impression. The seats

R OSE 'Félicité et Perpétue' tumbles over an arch. Foxgloves (*Digitalis purpurea*) are a classic biennial plant of English country gardens.

THE BANNERMANS love
imitating stone in oak,
and watching it weather and
crack as it ages.

are neatly, and rather cleverly, underplanted with box, reminiscent of another favourite Bannerman trick – that of including clipped ivy into the risers of steps. Oak is a material which the couple are very fond of, and they often work with it to represent stone, so that very Italianate features such as classical archways or pedestals are rendered in wood; "I love the way it weathers and changes over time," says Isabel.

The Bannermans are as prone to plant obsessions as other gardeners, which comes out particularly clearly in the dell garden. Isabel states out loud what many plant-focused designers feel: "There's a raft of plants we can't use in client's gardens – magnolias, for example." Magnolias illustrate many of the reasons that limit the use of certain plants: they are slow to flower, difficult and slow to propagate, and unavailable in large sizes. "I wish we had our own nursery," sighs Isabel – but the fact is that very few designers have the resources or the skills to run nurseries, and there are many reasons as to why a nursery, whose sole aim is to supply a designer, is simply not an economic proposition. There is a grove of tree ferns, and a great many other fern species around, even a startling, scarlet-painted, metal sculpture of unfurling fern fronds. The couple have, in the view of specialist Martin Rickard, played quite a major role in reviving interest in ferns amongst British gardeners.

What is particularly interesting about the Bannerman partnership is the degree to which tasks are shared – this is unusual amongst gardening couples, let alone among business partners. In talking to them about their work, the only hint of a difference is in their attitude towards tulips, which are a major feature of the garden in spring. Isabel says, "I like the sweet shop approach, bright colours, I'm mad about stripes, Julian thinks we should spend more time thinking them out, he loves 'Queen of the night'." But she does admit that "Julian has a particular flair for planting."

"I like creating gardens people can eat and live in," says Julian, "and I know when to stop gardening." It sounds as if here are two people who have not only had a very successful business career, but also know how to enjoy their lives – which comes across very strongly in their exuberant garden.

STONE WALLS, partly built of architectural salvage, shelter a swimming pool; in doing so, they also create a perfect environment for trapping scents – of roses, honeysuckles, liliesand heliotrope. Appreciation of scent is very dependent on the absence of any wind.

Some Favourite Plants

Philadelphus mock orange

"I love them for the scent," says Julian, "they are the one huge shrub that can be abandoned, and found healthy 20 years later. I love all those old Victorian varieties, and I like its neutralness the rest of the year when its not flowering." Philadelphus are large shrubs (varying between 1.5–4 x 2–4m/5–13 x 6½–13ft) with beautiful fragrance. They can be kept small with pruning, and can be trained against walls. Easy to grow in full sun or moderate shade. ZONES 3–6 MIN., DEPENDING ON SPECIES.

Roses

Julian says that in talking about roses he "feels like a serial adulterer, there are so many". 'Charles de Mills' is an easy and vigorous variety, with large flowers of red and purple (1.2 x 1.2m/ 4 x 4ft). 'Empereur de Maroc' is a dark crimson, with double flowers. 'Souvenir de la Malmaison' (shrub) is larger – 1.8 x 1.8m (6 x 6ft), with huge flowers and densely packed petals in blush pink (above); it is only a success in climates with a dry summer. ZONES 4–6 MIN., DEPENDING ON SPECIES.

Ferns

Matteucia struthiopteris is known as the ostrich fern, with very elegant upright fronds held in such a way as to give the plant a neat vaselike profile. It needs moist soils, in which it will spread by runners – an unusual habit for a fern. Usually grown in shade, but in higher altitudes this is unnecessary if there is plentiful moisture – 1 x 1.2m (3 x 4ft). ZONE 4 MIN.

Helleborus x *hybridus*

Helleborus x *hybridus* now comes in a wonderfully bewildering range of pinks, creams, dull reds, pale yellows and mysterious slatey grey-purples, some spotted, some plain, all invaluable for end of winter colour. The dark and glossy leaves are valuable for year-round interest too. They are easy in light shade, preferring fertile alkaline soils; good at coping with summer drought – 40 x 80cm (16 x 31in). ZONE 5 MIN.

Ribes odoratum

A little-known, wild currant, with yellow, clove-scented flowers in spring, it grows to 1.6m (5¼ft) tall and wide. "Let it grow into a big bush – all the better to scent the whole garden," says Julian. Good for underplanting with spring bulbs, especially as its habit is to be loose and open. Full sun or light shade. ZONE 3 MIN.

Daphne odora

This is the Bannerman's favourite of one of the most fabulously scented, hardy shrub genera, which slowly forms a mound of small evergreen leaves – 1.5m (5ft) high and across. The flowers are pale pink and are produced from mid-winter onwards. Like all *daphnes*, the plants need moist, but well-drained, alkaline soil. However, the plants are not long-lived. ZONE 7 MIN.

Sue Berger Bristol, UK

THIS IS ONE of the few gardens in this book that was occupied by the designer before he or she took up garden design. Inevitably, it has been a testing ground and the look that clients get when they commission Sue has been developed here. She came in 1974 when the existing 8 x 21m (26 x 69ft) garden had only "narrow beds down the sides, a few tiny fish ponds, plastic gnomes, and lawn." Its high walls and the mature trees in neighbouring gardens gave some privacy and character, but also cast shade. The long, rectangular shape is typical of many urban gardens, so lessons learned here are applicable elsewhere. It is also important to note that this is a house in a terrace of tall, Georgian houses, and creating a sense of seclusion has been vital.

Walls with plenty of climbers, some tall shrubs and a big miscanthus grass emphasise a strong vertical dimension, helping to make this garden seem bigger than it really is, and turning the sense of enclosure from urban claustrophobia into the intimacy of an arbour. Sue's division of it into separate areas, which you pass through in succession, from the gate at one end to the front door at the other, is a well-established design trick to develop the sense of a journey in a confined space.

ENCLOSED BY surrounding houses and trees, Sue Berger's garden is a true urban oasis, where box frames borders of perennials. A pergola of rebar seemingly invisibly supports a number of climbers in the background.

BIOGRAPHY There are certain images that become so often reproduced they become "iconic" – such has been the fate of a mirror in Sue Berger's garden she made and installed in 1997. As an intensely creative person, Sue has tried her hand at a number of different crafts; one, knitwear design, became a career; another, mosaic, remained a hobby. Sue's mosaic-bordered mirror seemed to crop up again and again in garden books and magazines. It somehow caught the zeitgeist of the moment – making exciting but homely gardens in small urban spaces; by reflecting image and light, mirrors can seem to increase the size of a garden.

The mirror was made in the earlier years of Sue's garden design career, in the mid-1990s. After a course in garden design at the English Gardening School in London, she went on to work with a colleague (Helen Phillips) to create gardens for clients in the south and west of England, including many in the centre of Bristol and Bath, where restricted space and often limited light can challenge both designers and plants.

Sue's garden style is very much about translating the 20th-century Arts and Crafts approach of balancing structure and effusive planting, into tight, and sometimes challenging, spaces. She likes using traditional elements, such as clipped box bushes or pleached limes, in places where designers used to a broader canvas might hesitate. Having created structure, Sue likes to fill in with a variation on a plant combination she has spent years refining, "the key thing is learning what works best together and for the time of year... what I love is lime, soft purples, magenta pinks, silver, very much a summer palette."

Fortunately, the kitchen and dining area on the ground floor open out directly onto the south-facing garden. Close to the house, there is a paved, sunken area with a table and chairs, and a climber-decked pergola helps to create a Mediterranean feel. Big clay pots are dotted about, some with ornamentals, such as agapanthus and *Teucrium fruticans*, others with salad crops and herbs, which can be almost picked from the kitchen door. An unusual, and distinctly contemporary, touch is a clump of the very tall grass, *Miscanthus sacchariflorus*.

The pergola is interesting, as it is made from rebar (the steel reinforcing rods used in heavy construction), an incredibly strong and versatile material, commonly used with great creativity in American gardens, but rarely seen in Europe. "We put it in about fifteen years ago," Sue recalls. "An architect friend, Jeremy Johnson-Marshall, designed and installed it, and it's now supporting a pale yellow *Rosa banksiae* 'Lutea', which flowers in early May, and a *Solanum crispum* 'Album', which flowers until November." She notes, "rebar keeps its strength so you can have a very narrow line"; it is very heavy, and is generally welded together, so specialist skills are needed to use it effectively and safely.

When she was an amateur gardener, Sue recalls, "I planted a *Rosa filipes* 'Kiftsgate' and a *Clematis montana*, both did 70ft (21m), they gave me huge confidence, but the Kiftsgate had to go when it started invading neighbouring gardens. I never looked at labels, so I made lots of mistakes.

A GARDEN dominated by green is so refreshing in the city. Box provides the structure, and evergreen shrubs with distinct foliage blur the walls, along with climbers. Perennials fill in all other spaces. The result is a balance of long-season structure and informal, even wild, and more seasonal flower colour.

OUTDOOR DINING makes
sense when the kitchen
door is only metres away.
This terrace area is beneath
the rebar pergola and
looks towards the rear of
the garden.

Then I started looking at gardens open to the public, like Sissinghurst and Hidcote. I began to build up an eye for plant combinations, and for old roses." The lawn began to shrink, as the planting beds expanded.

"For twenty years, though, it was all content, no form," Sue says. Things began to change in earnest when she started a course at the English Gardening School: "It was a one year correspondence course… I learnt a lot, which has shaped the garden, in particular, I learnt about form. We finally forfeited the lawn about fifteen years ago, and then I suddenly decided one weekend to make two rooms, keeping it very formal, with two huge central beds surrounded by paths." Sue then realised that she needed even more form, especially in winter, so in went some box hedging in the big beds. "It took three years to join up, then I added evergreen central statements: box balls in the corners, and box cones and a standard holly in the centre of the beds, and that looks really good," she says with finality, "and is how it will stay."

For a couple of years, one of the central beds was used for growing vegetables, but Sue found it "too shady, and I then got an allotment… so I just have a pot of salad leaves and herbs in the garden for that emergency lunch when you haven't anything else."

"Studying with the English Gardening School also got me thinking about shrubs," says Sue, "about their performance in particular… If they are only going to flower for two weeks, what about the rest of the year?" Seasonal interest is of key importance in small gardens, so Sue has always concentrated on long-performing species, and used a lot of bulbs for spring colour. Managing her own garden has taught her other useful design tricks too, such as combining scrambling herbaceous species with shrubs – "I've got a *Geranium psilostemon* climbing

through a *Rosa moyesii* 'Geranium'. The rose only flowers for two weeks; once it is over, the geranium carries on flowering and is supported by the rose." Since walls dominate Sue's garden, climbers are, inevitably, important. They contribute to its atmosphere of leafy luxuriance, and since it is possible to blend climbers relatively easily, they can do a lot to lengthen the season of interest.

Unlike many plant-orientated designers, Sue is not constantly seeking new plants. When a bamboo had to be removed, as it had begun to spread too aggressively – "it took us three weekends to remove it," she recalls – "it left a large bed, and I felt that I had enough experience to use stuff already in the garden to restock it. I bought nothing, just divided up favourite herbaceous plants, such as *Nepeta* 'Six Hills Giant', *Geranium psilostemon*, *Anemanthele lessoniana* and *Euphorbia robbiae*…

this confidence in my own resources had come from experience, which builds harmony". The important lesson here is that repetition of a few tried and tested plants can often create a far better impression than lots of novelties.

Small gardens are in some ways unforgiving, as everything is always visible. Maintenance is, therefore, crucially important. This may sound counterintuitive, but wild-looking gardens can take additional work, and certainly require more skill, than formal, controlled-looking ones. Likewise, the designer at home can take more risks. "I can go for chaos in my own garden," says Sue in respect of the difference between designing for clients and for herself. "I love an abundance. Chaos takes an enormous amount of garden editing, I probably spend eight hours a month from March to September doing this editing – weeding, pruning, cutting back, allowing new stuff to take over."

THE FAMOUS mirror, which lets in so much light to a dark part of the garden. Alongside is *Fatsia japonica*, an evergreen shrub that thrives in shaded city gardens, as well as adding an exotic touch.

Some Favourite Plants

Alchemilla mollis

This is a very familiar, early summer flowering perennial, whose lime-green flowers Sue rates highly for their ability to mix with a wide variety of other shades. Growing to 40 x 80cm (15½ x 31in), it is happy in sun or light shade, and needs reasonable soil moisture. In many gardens it self-seeds in borders and paving. ZONE 4 MIN.

Cistus x pulverulentus 'Sunset'

Sue says that she "loves anything Mediterranean, this cistus is a good one, as it doesn't grow too tall" – to about 60cm (23½in) high, spreading a similar amount. It has evergreen greyish foliage, and large deep pink to magenta flowers in early summer. Good drainage and sun is essential. Its toleration of drought (once established) and alkalinity mean that it is particularly successful in town gardens. ZONE 8 MIN.

Geranium x oxonianum 'Thurstonianum'

This is one of the many hardy geraniums that Sue says, "does very well in shade... and the colour really stands out in a shady patch." Growing to 60cm (23½in) in height with a spread of about 80cm (31in), the plant is covered in dark pink flowers with strange strap-shaped petals; the main flowering season is early summer, but there is always a further flush of flowers in late summer or early autumn. Sun or shade, but reasonable soil moisture is important. ZONE 5 MIN.

Luzula sylvatica 'Marginata'

Luzulas, or wood-rushes, are ideal plants for shade, including dry shade, and are particularly suitable for evergreen ground cover – "it creeps around, fabulous for infill, charming flowers, and looks so good next to ferns," says Sue. This variety has broad linear leaves, edged, ever-so delicately, with gold; the flowers are brown and appear in early summer. Growing to about 30cm (12in), plants should be spaced at 40cm (15½in) intervals for ground-cover purposes. ZONE 4 MIN.

Nepeta x faassenii 'Six Hills Giant'

This large-growing (60 x 80cm/23½ x 31in) version of catmint "flowers for weeks, and is very good in generously wide paths, softening their hard outline", according to Sue. It flowers in early summer, but if cut back, it flowers again in late summer/early autumn. Full sun, suitable for seasonally dry soils, although it may not repeat flower, if very dry. ZONE 3 MIN.

Santolina chamaecyparissus

"I don't like yellow flowers but put up with these for the sake of the beautiful silver foliage, and the neat button shapes formed by the buds," explains Sue. This mound-forming, evergreen, Mediterranean shrub grows to 60cm (23½in) and spreads to twice this size. Sun, drought-tolerant. ZONE 7 MIN.

John Brookes Denmans, West Sussex, UK

JOHN'S OWN GARDEN, Denmans, near Arundel in West Sussex, is 1.4 hectares (3 ½ acres) of lawn, trees and carefully orchestrated foliage. Wandering around on one bright June day, I felt that I was exploring a very different kind of garden to most of the gardens that I visit. I stress the word "wander", because it is a garden without any obvious axes or features to encourage a strong direction, which is emphasised by the flatness of the surrounding countryside, and by the fact that there are relatively few views out. It is remarkably restful. Striking plant forms were what struck me first, but not the fashionable spikiness of *phormiums* or yuccas. Particularly noticeable were perennials with strong shapes, such as *verbascums* (mulleins) with their distinctive rosettes and tall spires of yellow flowers, and various species of thistle-like *Eryngium*.

I remember John saying to me how he prefers to "work down from structure... colour is the last thing, a bonus." Yet the strong shapes never overwhelm, as they are a counterpoint to lots of 'mounds': hummocks of sage (*Salvia officianalis*), the low evergreen *Viburnum davidii*, or the roughly textured leaves of *Phlomis russeliana*.

The garden reminds me of a series of very open woodland glades, so when walking around I went from sun to shade and out to sun again,

A CURVING path sweeps towards the clocktower at Denmans. It can be seen in the distance, but its snaking route and intervening shrubs make it ambiguous – there is always a sense here of being enticed onwards.

BIOGRAPHY More than anyone else, at least in Britain, John Brookes MBE (born 1933) has helped to make garden design into a discipline, with his promotion of a professional body (the Society of Garden Designers), the writing of numerous books on the subject and his teaching – from 1980 to 1990 he ran a design school from his home at Denmans in Sussex. In addition, for many of us, his Chelsea Flower Show gardens from the 1960s onwards were our first introduction to contemporary garden design, to a design philosophy that had a direct link to many of the great names of 20th-century landscape design, such as Geoffrey Jellicoe (1900–96) and Thomas Church (1902–78).

"I design garden spaces," he says, "plants *per se* don't thrill me... my early experience working on the journal *Architectural Design* taught me that there had to be some sort of rules." His early books and show gardens stressed the architect's eye and, he now feels, over-emphasised structure, leading many of us (myself included) to associate his work with bricks and patios. "All I ever wanted to say was that there needs to be a structure in there, despite the fact that it might then be overlaid in plant material," he explains.

John did, in fact, start off his career in commercial horticulture, then worked for three years with Nottingham Parks Department, where he ended up in the design office. On leaving Nottingham, he worked for Brenda Colvin (1897–1981), who in the 1950s was one of Britain's most notable landscape architects. After a part-time university course, he moved on to the office of another big name, Sylvia Crowe (1901–97). It was after

this that he worked for *Architectural Design*. As a freelance designer, John has always balanced writing and lecturing with design work for clients scattered over many countries, including France, Germany, Italy, the USA, Japan, Chile and Argentina.

It is perhaps the very international range of work that has helped to bring about the most recent change in John's approach, that of paying great attention to what he calls the cultural element in horticulture, the importance of relating gardens to the local landscape, using native plant associations if at all possible – indeed John was one of the first designers to start experimenting with using native plants and wildflower meadow areas. "The world will begin to look the same if we all grow the same plants," he says.

with small groups of trees providing shady patches, but never so dense as to obstruct the view. Most of the trees are smaller species, or ones with light foliage, such as birches (*Betula* species), *Gleditsia triacanthos* or *Robinia pseudoacacia*, big enough to define spaces but always allowing views through at eye level, on to another open patch of garden beyond. The fact that there was little sense of direction didn't matter at all. In fact, it created a feeling that this garden could be explored by walking around in any direction whatsoever.

The blend of light shade and open areas reminds me of my limited experiences of exploring savannah environments, in Africa and in the United States, where there is a complex blend of wooded, open and in-between, transitional habitats over large areas. There is indeed a theory that because our species evolved

in the savannah, we are genetically predisposed towards feeling comfortable in savannah-like environments, such as classic English parkland[1]. Perhaps that explains the great atmosphere of peace I felt at Denmans. It is worth noting, however, that the light and shade here are not necessarily the result of human decisions, as major storms in 1987 brought down many trees.

John has lived at Denmans since 1980, but only actually bought it, with a business partner, in 1997. He came to live here because he liked it, and was a friend of Joyce Robinson, the then owner, who made the original garden with Bertie Read (her gardener). "Joyce was a plants woman," said John. "I tried to iron out the garden, making it into a simpler design." John, however, did not "take over" the garden, but increased his involvement gradually as Joyce grew older.

Joyce Robinson had been, in her own way, a real pioneer, aware before most other gardeners of the importance of understanding plant ecology. One of her design innovations was the rendition of a dry stream in gravel and pebbles, which sweeps through the garden to a pond at the southern edge of the garden. One of John's earliest design decisions was to add this real pool to act as a culmination to the gravel stream.

Interestingly, John has worked here in a very different way to how he would for a client. "I never made positive decisions, but I did put a pond in. Everything else has been piecemeal,"

he explains. "The garden changes by evolution rather than by making dramatic statements." This is how most gardeners develop their gardens over time, and perhaps should be a warning that sitting down and trying to design your own garden all in one go (perhaps while clutching one of John's books on design) is not necessarily such a good idea.

"Sweeping curves, rivers, ebb and flow, gravel paths, borders, lawn edges – no straight lines" are what I read in my notes. There is a boldness about the way that the borders and grass sweep round, but boldness does not always mean hard edges.

GRAVEL AT Denmans: conventional and well-graded between carefully positioned shrubs and a fine specimen of *Astelia nervosa* in some areas (left), more naturalistic, and less graded in others, alongside more spontaneous, and wilder-looking planting (right).

Plants have been allowed to self-sow into the gravel paths, or into the dry stream. This self-sowing blurs the boundaries between paths and border, yet in other places there are very clear boundaries. One particular place where boundaries are used to great effect is in the detailing of an area of lawn immediately outside John's house. The grass has been cut at two different heights, obviously over a very long time, so that there is a very definite contrast in texture and colour between the two. So simple, so effective, yet I had never seen this done anywhere else. According to John, "it originated when I made a low bank of rougher grass to hide the drive from the house." In another part of the garden a similar, but more conventional, effect has been created by leaving a large area of grass to grow as a wildflower meadow, ringed with conventionally short-mown turf. John Brookes' designs have always been seen very much as "contemporary"; he has never been one for designing traditional English gardens, "except tongue-in-cheek, when abroad." Yet it is interesting to note how few of those quintessentially contemporary plants and grasses he uses. He confesses that "I have problems with them, I can't make them work in design terms." That is something else that makes this garden special; it is very modern in feel, yet "grass-free". The lack of ornamental grasses and prevalence of rounded shapes makes it feel more Mediterranean.

Evergreen shrubs play an important role in the garden, as punctuation, usually as gentle mounds that define spaces. Huge "boulders" of box do this particularly effectively in the walled garden, providing an element of repetition, as they rise out of masses of perennials, including expansive self-sown clumps of evening primroses (*Oenothera* species) and the aromatic biennial sage, *Salvia sclarea* var. *turkestanica*.

I rapidly decided that I really loved the atmosphere at Denmans: it evokes the atmosphere of light and shade that many of us find deeply satisfying, but it is also an immensely stimulating garden, unconventional, but never feeling experimental or aggressively new. And, while John may not see himself as a "plants man", his understanding of the plants he uses is a large part of the beauty of the garden.

MULLEINS (this one is *Verbascum bombyciferum*) are profuse self-seeders, creating a striking effect *en masse* or dotted around other plants. Here they are in flower alongside yellow-green *Alchemilla mollis* in June.

Some Favourite Plants

"This question is totally at the other end of the spectrum to the way I think about plant material," says John. "I don't impose my favourites unless they are suitable, selection depends on location, orientation, soil, water availability and so on." He went on to explain that "favourites in *my* garden are of the garden forms of natives – the viburnums, verbascums, box and yew."

Choisya ternata

Neat evergreen leaves and a compact habit (to 1.8-m/5 ¾-ft high) have made this a very popular garden shrub. Fragrant white flowers in early summer are occasionally followed by a second flush a few months later. Needs shelter from cold winds, severe frosts, but shows some drought tolerance once established. ZONE 7 MIN.

Euphorbia characias subsp. *wulfenii*

Grey leaves and yellow-green flower heads in spring combined to make this a quintessential 'new' plant during the 1970s and 1980s. Its drought tolerance and reliability in any well-drained sunny site has, however, ensured a continuing popularity. The flower colour combines with purples and mauves to great effect. To 1.5m (5ft) high. ZONE 7 MIN.

Hydrangea arborescens 'Annabelle'

A medium to large spreading shrub (to 3 x 3m/10 x 10ft), with attractive light green leaves and very large heads of cream flowers in mid-summer. Best for moist soils, sun or light shade. A suckering habit makes it useful where a large space needs filling. ZONE 3 MIN.

Verbascum bombyciferum

Mulleins are a large genus of short-lived or biennial plants, mostly herbaceous. This species forms a wide rosette of broad white-felted leaves in its first year, sending up a 2m (6½ft) high spike of yellow flowers in the second, after which it dies, although it sets copious amounts of seed. Like most mulleins it thrives and easily re-establishes itself on poor stony soils – so it is particularly suitable for gravel gardens. ZONE 3 MIN.

Viburnum plicatum 'Mariesii'

A large sprawling shrub (to 3m/10ft high and across) whose attractively layered branching habit makes it a very useful species for year-round interest. The flowers are borne in spring, and like most viburnums consist of a head of small fertile florets and a showy ring of cream-coloured sterile florets. Pleated leaves give the plant an additional cachet. Sun or light shade on moist, well-drained soils. ZONE 5 MIN.

Roberto Burle Marx 'The *Sítio*', Santo Antonio da Bica, Brazil

I N 1949, Burle Marx bought an 80 hectare (198 acre) farm 45km (28 miles) from Rio, where he created a home, a garden, built a studio and developed a nursery. The nursery was used to propagate plants he had collected on his expeditions, in particular to grow enough of the ones that he wanted to use in design work. The farm, Santo Antonio da Bica, usually known simply as 'the *sítio*', became famous for its owner's lavish parties, often held in honour of visiting foreign guests. With its traditional long veranda, and slightly elevated position, the house is a wonderful place to escape the worst of the heat and to appreciate the lush surroundings.

Much of the property was left as forest, but several hectares around the house were developed as an ornamental garden, to which Burle Marx made constant adjustments over the years. What makes it interesting is how utterly different it is to anything he designed; it is much more traditional, intimate and personal, but somehow more alive, too. One of the problems Burle Marx was up against was that few of the wealthy, or corporate, clients he worked for had any knowledge of gardening, so horticultural management was left in the hands of staff. Given the low rates of pay in Brazil, it is possible to employ people to maintain gardens in a very intensive manner, the result of

S ALVAGED FROM the demolished buildings of Rio de Janeiro, granite blocks are home to a variety of bromeliads. They form a wall around a rectangular pond at one end of the oldest part of the garden.

BIOGRAPHY Roberto Burle Marx (1909–94) was one of the most important garden and landscape designers of the 20th century. He was raised in an artistically aware family of German heritage in Rio de Janeiro, and his story is a case of being the right person in the right place at the right time. Before Burle Marx, Brazil had no garden or landscape tradition of its own, only a colonial Portuguese one. After his death, there is little sign yet of anyone escaping his colossal shadow.

Burle Marx was an exuberant personality and compulsive creator. Trained as an artist, he continued to paint throughout his life (indeed he described himself as "painting with plants"), to make dramatic flower arrangements, and to design tiles, textiles and jewellery. From his first landscape design in c.1934, when he shocked the conservative burgers of Recife (in north-east Brazil) with a town square planted with locally native plants, to his death in 1994, he designed hundreds of gardens, parks, town squares, roof gardens and corporate landscapes. Unfortunately, few now survive in their original form. One that does, and which has become almost a national icon is the pavement at Copacabana in Rio, made in 1970, where abstract patterns in white, black and red stones run, dawdle and jog along the beachfront.

Two things made Burle Marx stand out as a garden designer: he was a fully paid-up member of the modern movement, and he was passionate about plants. His design work owed nothing to classical notions of geometry, and everything to the asymmetry of swirling organic shapes or jagged lines and angles.

The connection with abstract painting is usually very clear in his work, as it is with modernist architecture. Inevitably, he was drawn into the great 1960s project of Brasilia, the creation of a totally new capital city in the hinterland. Here, he worked with the architect Oscar Niemeyer, landscaping the grounds of the new government buildings.

From his first professional planting in Recife, Burle Marx was extremely inventive in his use of plants. Realising the immense botanical wealth of his homeland, Burle Marx sponsored expeditions into the hinterland to collect new species that he could use in his design work. In his later years he became very involved in the very uphill struggle to conserve the natural environment of Brazil – failure to make much progress caused him much heartache.

GARDENS OPEN TO THE PUBLIC

RIO DE JANEIRO
- Aterro de Flamengo (park)
- Banco Nacional Desenvolvimento Econômico Social (BNDES)
- Copacobana beach promenade
- Petrobras Building

BRASILIA
- Ministério das Relaçoes Exteriores
- Ministério da Justiça
- Ministério de Exército
- Tribunal de Contas da União

SÃO PAOLO
- Banco Safra, Rua Bela Cintra

which is that many feel extremely static and lifeless, much like a traditional bedding scheme. At the *sítio*, Burle Marx did as little or as much gardening as he wanted, so the result was much more homely, personal and alive.

The view of the garden from the house is of a lawn edged with borders and culminating in a pool – the lines are all much more traditional than his commissioned work. Probably Burle Marx took the geometry from the house, for this would have been one of the very few traditional buildings that he could have worked around. The pool is backed by blocks of granite, salvaged from 19th-century buildings that were being demolished in an orgy of destructive redevelopment in Rio, during the 1960s. Behind the house, a stretch of paving, shaded by large trees and a jade vine on a concrete pergola, is used for entertaining. A collection of

ceramic sculptures placed here are amongst the few artworks in the garden. The shade is a good place to get up close to a variety of ferns and other rainforest floor species. Large rounded pebbles are used as a dramatic mulch, a theme that is extended to other areas around the house. Out of them spring the plants Burle Marx collected: bromeliads, succulents, cycads, ferns, spearlike sansevierias, lush-leaved anthuriums and much more.

One of the main functions of the *sítio* garden was as a place to trial plants and to grow those that Burle Marx particularly loved. In his determination to use as many Brazilian native plants as he could, he was starting right at the very beginning; everything he used had to be assessed as being suitable for long-term cultivation. While the majority were grown in the nursery area, quite distinct to the garden, favoured species were grown

A POOL in the lower part of the garden is the perfect environment for water loving plants. A *Heliconia* variety (right) likes moist, but not wet, soil.

around the house, or in one of the other areas he developed on the property. The scenery around Rio is dominated by weatherworn granite that forms majestic rounded boulders; there are several places where Burle Marx used them as backdrops for planting. The big waterworn pebbles used around the garden echo the shapes of the boulders, and act as a foil for a wide variety of plant shapes.

When he worked on country gardens, Burle Marx always tried to blend the garden into the surrounding scenery. This he did at the *sítio* too, but with a greater degree of subtlety. He planted his own trees to join the natural forest growth on the hillside beyond the garden proper, and made a series of plantings in groves scattered around. The result is constant surprises when you walk up the slope, pausing to stop every now and again in the intense heat and humidity, as you come across plant groupings or individual plants that raise the question – does this grow here naturally or not?

The largest amount of open, unshaded ground is on the slope below the house and its relatively old-fashioned garden. Stone steps sweep down to a pool, and are surrounded by the unruly and sculptural

shapes of a variety of desert or dry habitat plants: *yuccas*, *euphorbias*, *pachypodiums*, *agaves* and *aloes*. Although Rio has plentiful rainfall, the importance of this dry-land flora to a garden designer in the humid tropics is actually quite important. The reason is that the natural flora is rainforest, and anything less than tree-sized is either going to grow in the deep shade of the forest floor or as an epiphyte on the tree branches, in dappled shade. Species that can survive the intense sunlight and dry winds experienced in unshaded conditions have to be sought from a different and drier climate zone.

Visitors to Brazil will inevitably experience Burle Marx's work in public spaces, and like all public spaces there is a lack of intimacy, and maintenance is often poor. Planting for all his work had to be kept simple for it to be maintained by relatively unskilled personnel – but in some ways that suited his artist's eye for boldly graphic detail. Only at the *sítio* do I feel that the real Burle Marx emerges; there is softness and pragmatism here. Of all his work that I have seen, this is the only place that felt to me like a real garden.

THE LONG verandah of the *fazenda* (ranch house) was home to many a party during Burle Marx's exuberant life. It looks out over a border-edged lawn which looks surprisingly conventional. The borders, however, were full of plants that he was actively trialling.

Some Favourite Plants

Alcantarea imperialis (Vriesia imperialis)

A large and dramatic bromeliad, up to 1.2m (4ft) across and high. The large rosettes live for several years before flowering, with a red and yellow spike, 2m (6½ft) high, after which they die, but they are usually succeeded by daughter rosettes. Moist soils and filtered sunlight. ZONE 12 MIN.

Setcreasea pallida 'Purple Heart'

Spreading herbaceous plant useful for ground cover – maximum height of 50cm (19¾in). Burle Marx used this alongside several other species to create large blocks of colour, often juxtaposing dramatically contrasting colours. It needs moist soil and protection from the hottest sun. ZONE 12 MIN.

Beaucarnia recurvata

The bunches of leaves that sprout out of the branches of this semi-desert shrub are soft in appearance, and a useful contrast to the stiffer and spikier shapes of yuccas and other plants from similar habitats. Eventually growing to 8m (26½ft), beaucarnias are suitable for seasonally dry soils and full sun. ZONE 12 MIN.

Hemerocallis varieties

Gardeners from temperate climes are always surprised to see how widely *Hemerocallis* (day lily) is used in sub-tropical or montane tropical regions. In such climates they are evergreen and are useful for 60cm- (2ft-) high ground covering as much as for their flowers. They need moist, but well-drained soil. Varieties bred for the tropics should be selected. ZONES 3–5 MIN, DEPENDING ON SPECIES.

Anthurium species

The *anthuriums* we are most familiar with are exuberant "flamingo flowers". Most species have undistinguished flowers, but handsome and expansive foliage. Burle Marx used several that he collected himself in the rain forest. All varieties need year-round moisture, humidity and shade. ZONE 12 MIN.

Tibouchina urvilleana

A small tree in its native Brazil, this makes a good, long-flowering conservatory plant in cooler climates. These trees appear in several Burle Marx gardens – left behind from forest clearance. The foliage is evergreen, with distinctive veining, and densely hairy – attractive enough when out of flower. If grown indoors, frequent pinching-out or pruning is necessary to avoid leggy growth. Full sun in cooler climates, semi-shade in the tropics. ZONE 12 MIN.

Tracy DiSabato Aust The garden at Hiddenhaven, Columbus, Ohio, USA

I n 1987, when Tracy and her husband Jim Aust moved into their log-cabin house, the 1000 sq m (¼ acre) garden appeared to have little to offer, and a heavy clay soil was not a promising start. Now 3000 sq m (¾ acre) in size, it is burgeoning with exuberantly happy plant life, numerous colourful works of art, and chickens.

"Initially," says Tracy, "I planted up with left-over plants from research I had been doing at Ohio State University… I had been chilling plants in freezers to see what survived and what didn't… the survivors ended up in my garden, so they were a hardy lot." Winters here are cold – down to -28°C (-18°F). "At first I planted mostly perennials," she recalls, "but recently I have got more interested in woody plants, so now I'm putting in more conifers and shrubs. I'm realizing more and more how shrubs complete a garden, giving it structure and a longer season… when I started gardening there were hardly any perennials, and certainly no grasses, now there has been such a change in fashion." Shrubs and small trees are also a way to incorporate plenty of the fall colour for which the northeastern United States is famous. Fundamental to all of her gardening is "to use common plants in less common ways, and to mix the familiar and the unfamiliar."

Yellow *Rudbeckia fulgida* var. *speciosa* is deservedly one of the most popular garden plants of North American origin – useful for its compact habit and long-flowering season. Tracy's great discovery is that taller perennials can be 'pruned' to do what this plant does naturally.

BIOGRAPHY Few can match Tracy DiSabato Aust (born 1959) for sheer energy – mental and physical; as if the labour involved in gardening is not enough, Tracy is also a triathlete, competing at international level. She is one of the best-known speakers on the international garden lecturing circuit, largely because of one very influential book, *The Well-Tended Perennial Garden* (Timber Press, 1998). This outlines an innovative range of techniques for the management of garden perennials, mainly through well-timed and judicious pruning. Their development illustrates something very important about Tracy – that she is a genuine researcher in a way very few other garden writers are. She is, however, first and foremost a garden designer.

Tracy studied Horticulture at The Ohio State University, after which she spent two years working in gardens in Europe, first at Kalmthout Arboretum in Belgium and then at Knightshayes in England, where the head gardener was Michael Hickson, one of the most highly-regarded of his profession at the time; "he used to walk me round the garden every morning... I learnt so much from him", Tracy recalls.[1] On her return to the United States, Tracy took a graduate programme, researching plant hardiness, and then began teaching horticulture. Her garden design career had, however, started earlier, as she had begun to advise people on their gardens while still an undergraduate.

Tracy describes how, in her early days, she "got a team of women together and a couple of men for the heaviest work. We'd do the planting, and then later the maintenance as well... my husband's a dentist, but if he had time off, he'd come and join us too." Since then,

plant selection and maintenance have become the core of Tracy's work – she still does design hard landscaping but sub-contracts its installation. Around about the time of the birth of her son Zac in 1989, she started writing about gardening, using her experience with plants in her own and her clients' gardens as raw material; this led to lecturing to garden clubs, which now fills her schedule.

GARDENS OPEN TO THE PUBLIC

- **Plantings in the Chadwick Arboretum** at The Ohio State University, Columbus, Ohio.

- **The Entrance Walk Perennial Bed,** Inniswood Gardens, Westerville, Ohio.

Tracy's garden design career is, in fact, only one part of a wider set of creative interests, as she does watercolour painting and likes to buy or commission artworks for the garden. Several brightly coloured glass works are dotted around; she explains, "I met a young glass blower, he was doing pieces for interiors, but I wanted work which would survive out of doors, so we worked on designs together." Tracy also commissioned an Amish carpenter to make a bench with a gap for a tile inlay, which was made by her art teacher. "Artworks add to a garden," says Tracy, "and they are also so useful when the garden is having a bad hair day, they can bring colour into an area." She sees her garden as "eclectic", but tries to develop a sense of continuity by repeating colours in various structures across the garden.

Chickens have been a feature of life at Hiddenhaven since 2003, but they only have free run in the garden later in the season, "when everything is well established; otherwise they can do damage," says Tracy. "I used to do a whole big vegetable garden," she says, "but deer here are a big problem, so now I tend to do just a few ornamental vegetables, such as Redbore kale, Bulls Blood beetroot and ornamental lettuce."

Like many American gardeners, Tracy has had a go with establishing prairie perennials, but germination on her heavy soil limited its success. She has, however, been able to slowly build up a natural-looking meadowy area to the side of the pond, which had been dug in the early years of making the garden, "scattering seed from deadheaded perennials, sowing annuals like

1 Both are exceptional gardens: Kalmthout is one of the greatest private arboretums in Europe, Knightshayes is a woodland garden laid out in the early to mid 20th century – it is now owned by the National Trust.

ID-TO late-summer
is the high point for
perennials in many open
North American habitats
and gardens. Whereas
traditionally they were grown
in wide borders, narrow
paths like this may be a
better way to experience
them, as it allows us to be
surrounded by flowers. Trees
and shrubs are an important
part of the backdrop,
particularly for spring and
autumn interest.

poppies and cornflowers… there is now a good mix of natives and non-natives."

Tracy's book on perennial management made an impact because it was genuinely innovative, and based on years of empirical research, most of which had been done here, "so the garden has to be a living laboratory, but it has to be for the family as well." Tracy practises what she preaches, "I still

do a lot of perennial pruning, either cutting back late season species or early ones post flowering. …I prefer to cut back than to stake… with some plants it is now automatic that I cut back, such as *Heliopsis helianthoides*, but others I leave for their structure, such as the big *eupatoriums* (Jo Pye weeds)… I don't prune for winter, as I find that leaving dead stems improves survival."

Some Favourite Plants

Acer griseum

The profusely peeling, cinnamon-coloured bark of this small (12m/ 40ft high) tree is the main reason for growing it, but Tracy sees other good reasons – "I like to use it as a specimen in gardens, it's slow and its multi-season." Its autumn colour is rich scarlet and crimson. Best grown out of cold winds, it dislikes dry soils, but is otherwise easy. ZONE 4 MIN.

Allium schubertii

One of several dramatic allium species that Tracy likes to use as spring or early summer flowering bulbs. The violet to pink flowers open out on stems to form a veritable firework of a flower head (to 60cm/ 23in), which later hardens to a stiffly decorative and long-lived seed head. "Some people spray paint them," notes Tracy. Like many bulbs from the Middle East, this one will not reliably re-flower, needing very sunny and dry conditions in order to do so. ZONE 5 MIN.

Angelica gigas

This biennial with large purple-flushed flowers in summer, and deep purple-red, rounded flower heads makes a dramatic sight. "It's architectural and sculptural," says Tracy, "I like to grow it with grasses, especially *Calamagrostis brachytricha*." Growing to 2m (6 ½ft), it dies after flowering, but scatters seed, which may germinate; where this does not occur, seed should be collected and sown immediately in trays of seed compost. Likes sun or very light shade, fertile soils. ZONE 5 MIN

Calamagrostis brachytricha

A 1m (3ft) high grass that produces delicate, fluffy flower/seed heads in late summer, topping off stems that radiate elegantly out from a tight base of narrow, fresh, green leaves. "Good in light shade," says Tracy; "I love it for verticality and form." Any well-drained soil is suitable; sun is necessary in more northerly climates than the continental USA.
ZONE 7 MIN.

Itea virginica

Dramatic in flower, this deciduous shrub astonishes with its 10cm (4in) long stiff "catkins" of pale green, honey-scented flowers, which are produced in early summer. In autumn it turns orange and red. Tracy says, "I include it in almost any design as it'll do anywhere – sun, shade, wet, dry, clay." Height is up to 3m (10ft).
ZONE 5 MIN.

Papaver orientale 'Patti's Plum'

Tracy loves the mysterious dark purple colour of this oriental poppy variety. Like all these perennial poppies, it flowers in early summer but its foliage dies back by mid-summer. "I don't see this as a problem," says Tracy, "as we often get re-growth, and I like to leave the seed heads, but I also oversow with annual poppies like the opium varieties." Height is about 70cm (27½in). Full sun and good drainage. ZONE 3 MIN.

Christine Facer Througham Court, UK

THE FIRST SIGHT of Througham Court might be enough to make you think that you had come to the wrong address – it is almost a parody of English, picture-postcard perfection, an ancient (1610) Cotswold stone house perched on the side of a secret Cotswold valley, with terraces studded with enormous topiary yew and box, surrounded by a verdant scene of pasture and trees. The main entrance, however, is through the "Anatomy of a Black Swan" gate, which is enough to convince anyone that this is no ordinary garden (or garden owner). The gate is a visual metaphor for what the financial market trader and writer Nassim Taleb calls "black swans": rare,

unpredictable events that have massive impact (good or bad). The jet-black gate is beautifully made (by a Scottish ironworker); the fact that black swans usually mean trouble is emphasised by a short stretch of barbed wire crudely wrapped around one corner.

The black swan signifies what makes this garden special – artistically designed, very well executed sculptures and installations that illustrate particular scientific concepts. The extraordinary and slightly surreal aspect is that they are all shoehorned into such a wonderful example of English, Arts and Crafts garden design. The garden was laid out by architect

CLIPPED YEWS, striped lawns and a landscape of fields and woods is quintessentially southern England. Yet within this traditional framework Christine has made a series of cutting-edge garden installations. The red is *Papaver orientale* 'Beauty of Livermore'.

BIOGRAPHY "I felt I needed a new challenge", says Dr Christine Facer (now in her fifties), about her decision in 1999 to enrol on a landscape-design course. A mid-life career change is not unusual, but to jump into it from the peak of one's previous career, with only a week in between, definitely is – but there is a feeling that Christine never stops. A malaria researcher of international renown, she has been president of the British Society for Parasitology, and sat on the Council of the Royal Society of Tropical Medicine and Hygiene. "Science has been my life," she says, "I started with a year at art school, but it was not for me and I decided to follow up my scientific interests instead."

Christine's work as a garden and landscape designer has, with only a few exceptions, been for private clients – the small, London gardens that are the mainstay of many designers' careers and a number of country properties. She has designed a number of roof terraces for businesses, and of the country properties she has designed, two feature amphitheatres. The first public work will be a landscape for a new Maggie's Centre (Maggie's Cotswolds) in Cheltenham. Maggie's Centres are cancer help and advice centres named after the late Maggie Keswick, a landscape designer, best known for the vast, grass mounds at her family home in Scotland, now occupied by her husband, the architectural theorist, Charles Jencks.

Christine could also be described as working in the currently fashionable field of "conceptual" garden-making, where ideas are central to the design. However, unlike much conceptual gardening, which verges on

installation art, no-one is left in any doubt that Christine has actually made a garden. Her designs include the "Genetic Garden" for the first International Festival of the Garden at Westonbirt (England) in 2002, "Virus Dynamics" for the Chaumont Festival of Gardens 2004, and "Paternity Suite" for a British television garden programme in 2005.

GARDENS OPEN TO THE PUBLIC

- **Maggie's Centre,** Cheltenham, Gloucestershire, UK (completion 2010–11)

- **Throughham Court** garden is open to groups by appointment.

Norman Jewson (1884–1975) in the early 1930s, and incorporates many of the features that made this immensely influential style so distinctive: dry stone retaining walls, terraces, topiary and a sunken garden. In spring, the historic and traditional character is emphasised by mass bulb planting: "Every year I plant five to six thousand tulips," Christine explains; this is clearly not the garden of an ascetic intellectual.

As with many Arts and Crafts gardens, individual spaces are created by compartments, usually defined by hedges, and often referred to as rooms. This makes it very much easier to keep each conceptual installation separate – a common failing of many theoretical or other intellectual gardens is that installations or other features run into each other. There is a Cosmic Evolution Garden, a Chiral Terrace (inspired by the left- and

right-handedness of many drugs and "mirror molecules"), an Entry into Chaos Gate (Chaos Theory) and several features that evoke the 13th-century Italian mathematician, Leonardo Fibonacci, whose number sequence underlies many of the patterns to be found in nature.

Each installation in the garden is concerned with illustrating, artistically, a key concept in science. "In clients' gardens," Christine explains, "I use a scientific approach but it is not always obvious. I normally take one idea for a garden commission – for example, a recent project includes an open-air theatre, with the design based on the Golden Section and stepped in accordance with the Fibonacci series. At Throughham there is a multitude of ideas. "I try to visualize science in a different context, I present a scientific idea and then make an image into an art form, maybe

THE Chiral Terrace
addresses the enigmatic
issue of certain compounds
vital to the chemistry of
life being 'left-' or 'right-
handed'. The materials are
polished black granite, white
Portuguese limestone and
red acrylic.

metaphorical." Charles Jencks, she recalls, once said, "garden art is a genre close to autobiography, so this garden is a narration of my scientific interests, a book to be read." Jencks is, in fact, a good friend and "as my mentor, he frequently critiques what I do."

What this garden is not, however, is simply a collection of clever artworks, as Christine insists, "I like everything to have a function, I am not a great believer in 'art placed in the garden', even the cosmic spheres are seats"; the cosmic spheres are six Ancaster stone balls in the Cosmic Evolution Garden, which represent planets, each one inscribed with one of the six numbers that

govern the evolution of the universe. Christine also emphasizes that the mathematics is not just there for intellectual satisfaction, but that "patterns in nature are mathematically governed." The logic of this is that by using number sequences in the way she places plants Christine can create effects subtly different to those that are "expected": "trees at an exact spacing are dull compared to placing them at distances dictated by a number sequence." As an example, in the field beyond the boundary of the garden is a snaking line of birch (*Betula utilis* var. *jacquemontii*) — rather than space them equally, which is what we tend to be conditioned to do, they are planted at

STEPS OF red Astroturf© jolt the visitor out of their complacency and, of course, they never have an off-day. *Cordyline australis* 'Purpurea' lines the steps, while 'drumstick alliums' (hybrids of *Allium giganteum*) adorn the borders above in late spring.

intervals based on the Fibonacci series. The effect is to foreshorten perspective, so that the trees look as if they are at a greater distance from the viewer than they really are.

Those parts of the garden that illustrate scientific knowledge or theories are sure to make an impact on anybody; they are highly graphic, beautifully made and can involve some startling colours – "Black, white and red is a favourite combination," says Christine. Their complete understanding can involve so much interpretation for the non-scientist, however, that their immediate impact is lost. Such a criticism cannot be said of Christine's planting designs for clients; she loves colour, "I use the garden as a laboratory to experiment with colour combinations before trying them in clients' gardens." On my springtime visit, a "rusty" border was just beginning to get into its stride, with orange 'Ballerina' tulips amidst clumps of annuals and perennials that would provide oranges and dark reds for the rest of the season: varieties of *Achillea, Kniphofia, Eremerus,* species of *Digitalis,* the yellow *Rudbeckia maxima* and the rich brown of *Helenium* 'Moerheim Beauty'. Interestingly, towards the latter half of the season, Christine likes to include some blues "to provide a lift", such as *Salvia* 'Blue Denim', *Salvia farinacea* 'Victoria', and the pretty Chinese forget-me-not, *Cynoglossum amabile.* This planting combines annuals with perennials; Christine is very fond of using annuals, with a greenhouse in the kitchen garden full of young plants in pots and trays waiting to go out once the danger of frost is past. Such a use of annuals is untypical of designers – for it is very difficult to specify their use in clients' gardens for obvious reasons, and a love of them is rarely expressed in the designers' own gardens.

An area with particularly exuberant colour in spring is the "Zigzag Arboretum", where Christine grows what she describes as "my favourite trees, and there isn't much space, so they are rather packed together." Birches, Japanese maples, a *Paulownia tomentosa,* a *Davidia involucrate,* a fastigiate *Liriodendron* and several more are cheerfully underplanted with hellebores, tulips, *Allium nigrum* and the towering *Angelica archangelica.* This really feels like someone is having fun, growing particular plants because they love them, just for the sake of them, and without feeling the need to make them fit

into a particular design or context. Througham Court is an extraordinary garden. Bold – brought home most graphically by a set of steps covered in red Astroturf©, which must bring many a garden visitor up short. "It adds colour in winter and prompts you to look at what lies beyond." What is unusual is that Christine's highly intellectual garden installations are slipped confidently into a framework and a context from a completely different era. The Arts and Crafts era is one that has become so familiar – to the point of becoming a cliché. Here, radical juxtapositions defy the complacency of assumption, and make for a garden of thought and continuing surprises.

A PLANTING of 'hot' colours. Combinations like this in the garden are used by Christine for evaluation purposes, before she risks them in clients' gardens. Note the pale blue *Perovskia atriplicifolia* – its addition serves to lift the entire composition, which might otherwise be oppressively dark.

Some Favourite Plants

Actaea simplex 'Brunette'

"The flowers are like shooting stars against a dark background of *Ophiopogon planiscapus* 'Nigrescens'. I leave the stems to stand all winter – they look architectural and the seed heads are a favourite of birds," says Christine of this tall (1.5m/5ft) perennial, with wonderfully scented, cream flowers and dark brown leaves. It needs a cool spot, with shade and a well-drained, but constantly moist, soil, and thrives in full sun at northerly latitudes. ZONE 4 MIN.

Sanguisorba officinalis and *S.tenuifolia* varieties

With handsome divided foliage, these mid to late-summer flowering perennials produce spires of deep red bobbles or fluffy catkin-like flowers, depending on the species. Growing to around 1.5–2m (5–6ft) tall, they are easy to grow, thriving in sunny positions with a moist soil. Their tall and rangy stems have a 'see-through' quality, which means that although large they never dominate. ZONE 4 MIN.

Lilium regale

One of the deliciously best lilies for scent, this species is also long-lived and can even self-seed in moist, but well-drained, soils. Frequently grown in pots, Christine notes, "it works well in borders, coming back better the following year. Growing to about 1m (3ft) tall, this lily needs sun and is best grown in groups. ZONE 5 MIN.

Persicaria amplexicaulis 'Firedance'

"*Persicarias* are most versatile, and this one goes on flowering for such a long time," says Christine, of this unusually bushy growing perennial. At 1.2m (4ft) high and spread, this is a useful plant for filling space at the front of larger borders and for providing colour (a dark red) from August to October. Moist to average soils, sun or light shade. ZONE 4 MIN.

Digitalis ferruginea 'Gigantea' and *D.parviflora*

"I like plants for their shape as well as colour," Christine points out; while the common *D. purpurea* is very bright, other species tend to be in soft yellows, fawns and browns. The flowers of *D. ferruginea* are particularly subtle, but arrayed on the most elegantly slender and tall stems. Enjoys full sun and good drainage, short-lived, but self-sowing on lighter or stony soils. ZONE 4 MIN.

Agrostemma githago 'Ocean Pearl'

An annual with a flowering season of about a month, this white form is, Christine notes, "such a pretty flower that mixes well with taller plants." Slender at about 1m (3ft) high, it is best incorporated into borders alongside perennials for support, rather than grown with other annuals. If left to self-seed it will, generally, self-sow. Sun.

Nancy Goslee Power Santa Monica, California, USA

THIS GARDEN is for living. I live outside, it is an extension of the house, I eat, read and do everything outside, and I live with five animals, a pug and four cats – they're doglike cats," Nancy explains. In a climate where the extremes of cold and heat are rare, living so much of one's life outside is an option that the rest of us can only dream about. Thomas Church, the Californian landscape architect who created the concept of the garden as an extension of the house, would have approved.

That Nancy's garden is so small and urban makes it more roomlike – there are two garden areas, the back, which is about 50 sq m (538 sq ft), and the front 30 sq m (323 sq ft). She describes it as "early 1900s", and says, "it was a complete shack when I got it, so I had it torn down and built a new one on the old footprint, but it is tiny, inspired by little houses in Brazil, just one big room really. I'm always tempted to move, but it is a spectacular location. It's in "baja" (lower) Santa Monica, part of the Los Angeles conurbation... I like the cool climate, I'm near the beach, and I'm one block from funky Venice. I like the edginess of LA."

As might be expected, walls tend to dominate – they are coloured with the ochre colour often associated with traditional buildings in climates

OCHRE WALLS are warm but never dazzling – important in warmer climates. Mirrors reflect light and help to create an illusion of greater space, while ferns are perfect for the reduced light of an urban garden.

BIOGRAPHY Originally an interior designer, Nancy Goslee Power (born 1942) has also worked in publishing, having been a contributing editor for *House Beautiful* and *House and Garden*. However, the pull of the great outdoors proved stronger, "as I have come from a long line of women farmers and gardeners", so in 1981 she set up a landscape design company. Her work includes public, commercial and residential landscapes, with participation at every stage of the process from planning down to detailed planting.

Nancy is unusual in the American landscape industry in having come to landscape design through gardening – "I love, love, love plants and trees, I'm happiest outside." She insists on the importance of a real and personal engagement with landscape – "I went to art school in Florence. In learning about landscape the world has been my school, I love travelling and just looking."

It is difficult to pin down Nancy's work to a particular style, as she believes, "I don't think my work is different to what other landscape architects do, it is more about being harmonious... I relate to the land and the architecture of the building." Sustainability has always been a part of her practice, although she does not shout about it, "I started using spiky plants, like agaves and aloes, ages ago; they are part of the look of the climate, people used to grow them, but had forgotten about them, and started to grow things like tree ferns and azaleas, which need more water." As she points out "there is just no water here, period, our rainfall is just 10in (25cm) per year)". Many of the best drought-tolerators are not, however, natives. Nancy explains, "I'm not a native plant nut, I love all plants... there's no such thing as a bad plant, only a plant in the wrong place."

Among Nancy's influences she mentions Roberto Burle Marx for "his love of plants... he taught me not to be afraid to use large masses of plants, and go for big patterns, go bolder, go bigger." Although she gains ideas and inspiration from everywhere she travels, Japan has been a particular inspiration.

Given that many in the garden and landscape design profession feel that they are not taken seriously by architects and designers in other fields, it is interesting to note that Nancy was commissioned by Frank Gehry, one of the world's leading architects, to design his own garden.

with bright sunshine, along with some vivid blues. Planting is limited for a number of reasons and the soil is difficult. "It's an old sand dune with very sharp drainage," explains Nancy. "There is very little temperature change, so plants often don't perk up... my neighbour has some trees that really shade me, so it is rather a green garden... but I use a lot of plants in pots to provide colour, and a living theatre – they keep me amused."

The plants with the most impact are the king palms (*Archontophoenix cunninghamiana*) whose elegant grey trunks appear almost as pillars, and a *Cupressus cashmeriana*, a cypress whose pendant blue-grey foliage is often regarded as the most beautiful of any in the genus. "I am still experimenting with native ferns," says Nancy. "I don't even know the names of some of them, but they do really well, and tree ferns, geraniums and pelargoniums also do well. Anything from the Canaries thrives here, and a few South African things." The reality is that most plants have annual biological cycles, and that without variation, physiological mechanisms are upset and they grow poorly as a result. The Atlantic Islands (Canaries, Azores, Madeira) and part of the South African Cape are amongst the few other areas in the world with a similar balmy, "non-climate", so it is not surprising that species from these areas flourish.

To bring life to her green garden, Nancy uses a lot of bulbs in containers, particularly South African ones. "My neighbour has a fence, and I painted my side of it blue, an idea from Morocco," she explains. "Anything hot and pink looks good against it... I like *Scilla peruviana*, it does well, and flowers for ages.

Ｋing palms are read as
columns around the
kind of formal pool which
seems almost *de rigeur* in
warm climates. Pots allow
maximum flexibility for
splashes of colour to be
introduced as and when
necessary. The shrub
with pendant white
trumpets (right) is
Brugmansia suaveolens.

NANCY GOSLEE POWER   73

Some Favourite Plants All of these plants are notably drought-tolerant, once established.

Agave attenuata

This is one of the most beautiful of this quintessentially desert climate genus. Tapering blue-grey leaves give it elegance and are a good foil for many other plants. With time the plant develops a distinct trunk – to 1.5m (5ft) high, and suckers. It is more tolerant of light shade than many agaves and appreciates a more fertile and moister soil than others. ZONE 9 MIN.

Arbutus 'Marina'

The "strawberry trees" are highly distinctive, with dark evergreen leaves, an open habit and cinnamon-coloured bark. This one is particularly vigorous, with attractive, reddish, young foliage; pale pink flowers are produced at various times throughout the year, but especially in winter, when they can be quite spectacular – to 15m (50ft) high. Full sun and lime-free soils are preferred. ZONE 8 MIN.

Euphorbia characias subsp. wulfenii

This grey-leaved perennial is invaluable for its presence in winter and its large heads of yellow-green flowers in early spring, a colour that serves to enhance the brighter tones of spring bulbs. Growing to about 1m (3ft) high and across, the fleshy stems are replaced annually, so although it never dies back like a conventional perennial, it does need a mid-summer tidy-up. Full sun or light shade (including dry shade). ZONE 8 MIN.

Helleborus argutifolius

Grown for its majestic, greyish, leathery foliage, rather than for its pale green flowers, this perennial tends to look its best during the Mediterranean winter – further north it is a valuable evergreen addition to a border. The soft colour combines well with early spring flowering bulbs. Likes full sun or light shade; in rich soils it can become top-heavy and fall over. ZONE 7 MIN.

Lavendula x heterophylla

With greener leaves than most lavenders, and a relatively upright and tall (to 1.2m/4ft) habit, this species is particularly distinctive; it is notably reliable in warmer climates (and less suitable for cooler ones). The flowers are blue-violet and are held on tall stems well clear of the foliage. Enjoys full sun. ZONE 8 MIN.

Pittisporum crassifolium 'Compactum'

Thick, glossy, evergreen leaves look good all year round, and they indicate that this New Zealand shrub is resistant to salt-laden, coastal winds; indeed it is reckoned to be the toughest of the pittosporums. Small maroon flowers in spring produce a distinct and pleasant fragrance in the evening. This form only grows to 1m (3ft) high and wide, whereas the species forms a large shrub to 6m (19½ft) high. Likes full sun. ZONE 8 MIN.

Naila Green Dawlish, Devon, UK

ONE OF THE MOST nonsensical things that is occasionally heard in Britain is the statement, "It's so difficult to make a garden at the coast." It is an extraordinary that the British, despite our self-image as being an "island' race" and as "the world's leading gardening nation", are so incapable of making good, coastal gardens. The usual ploy is to plant a massive windbreak, and then garden away, pretending that the sea isn't there. Anyone who complains about the difficulties of seaside gardening should go and visit Naila's garden.

Here is a garden that is literally on the coast: it stands at the edge of a cliff that drops down to the beach at the head of a broad bay, and to the west the red sandstone cliffs stretch away to a dramatic rock arch on a headland. "This garden is about the view," says Naila, but the wind can be fierce and persistent – this, combined with the high level of sunlight, can mean plants become desiccated very quickly. The soil is very poor, an acidic sand, but Naila points out that there are advantages: "You can dig into it so easily, which makes light of transplanting, and you can make new borders and paths so quickly."

Stepping outside the house, you are confronted by a dense mass of multi-textured, multi-hued growth – mostly tough evergreens, species

THE WINDBLOWN shape of the shrubs in the rear of this picture illustrates how strong the wind is in Naila's garden. Here, varieties of *Lavandula*, *Crocosmia* and *Euphorbia* thrive; all are from climates we associate with warmth – illustrating the fact that coasts are not necessarily cold and that physical resilience is more important than hardiness.

BIOGRAPHY Naila Green (1951) is a good example of a designer firmly rooted in her region. Although she designs in other parts of Britain, most of Naila's work is in the southwest. Apart from frequent storms, this is one of the best gardening climates in Europe, with plentiful rain throughout the year and mild winters. Nurseries, both wholesale and retail abound, and so Naila is able to make use of a wide range of plants.

Born in the Belgian Congo, to parents of Indian heritage, Naila came to Britain as a refugee when she was a child, with no tradition of gardening in the family. She describes herself as starting "a career as a graphic designer, then I was an art teacher... I had a family... then started gardening, I got completely hooked, I remember a week I spent visiting National Trust gardens, when I just learnt so much." She did a design course, started work as a designer and then built a show garden at the first Hampton Court Flower Show' in 1989. She carried on building show gardens, including a total of twelve at Hampton Court, three at Chelsea and some regional ones. "I used to teach at Bicton College," she says, "I did quite a few of the shows with students... I did shows for twelve years, and then I had so much work, I had to give them up." Most of her work is for private clients, but she has also done some corporate work; much of it is in coastal locations.

with leathery straplike leaves or dense twiggy shrubs. There is a sense that all the plants are supporting and sheltering each other, and that, without constant clipping back, the tide of vegetation would soon overwhelm the paths and small, decked areas, which Naila has made for sitting out.

In conventional gardening, carefully spaced plants can be vulnerable if they are unsupported and exposed to the full force of the sun and the wind. What Naila has done is to replicate the dense intertwining of the natural vegetation of environments such as English heaths, Mediterranean maquis or South African Cape fynbos. "I like," she says, "a bulk of plants, so that they shelter each other. In fact, some plants like astrantias depend on the shelter of others to survive... and the plants dead leaves automatically self-mulch, so that the soil gets better over time."

Naila and her husband Ian (who is also part of her design business) live in a very average English 'semi' (i.e. semi-detached – sharing a wall with their neighbours), but the land that comes with the house gives them their own stretch of coastline. The area in front of the house is only a small part of the garden here, which stretches further up the hill, extending to an acre (4,046 sq m) – although much of this is wild bracken and gorse-clad cliff top, which Naila knows she will never get around to cultivating. Holm oak trees (*Quercus ilex*) and the evergreen *Viburnum tinus* provide a sheltered parapet part of the way up; there is a vantage point where you can get the sense of poking your head up above the vegetation for a particularly good view of the coast. Further up still is a pine tree with montbretia (*Crocosmia* x *masonorum*) spiralling in towards its trunk — "it symbolises a snail, which has always been Ian's nickname for me, the two seats here give me my favourite view, directly to Thatcher's Rock" (the arch on the horizon). In fact, there are lots of secret sitting areas, Naila explains. "The design

1 Now run by the Royal Horticultural Society, this event, always held in July, is now the second most important event in the British gardening calendar, after Chelsea.

NAILA HAS discovered that the key to success with coastal vegetation is to imitate the dense intertwined growth of the plant communities which naturally flourish in exposed places. Successful species typically have compact twiggy growth or leaves that are obviously physically tough – like phormiums, with their leathery strap-shaped leaves.

evolves from places to sit, which use the topography to get the best views but also give shelter." Part of the house is sometimes let out for holidaymakers, so creating private areas for both them and for Naila and Ian is also a factor in the planting and management of screening shrubs.

Naila and Ian carved the newer areas of the garden out in 2006, which included clearing gorse and brambles for three months. Ian has a small vegetable garden, and Naila is creating many new plantings, although sandy soil and

strong winds tend to slow down progress. Naila describes herself as "always having been a 'plantaholic'… it's all about plants." In addition, there are other reasons why hard landscaping features are limited: not only are the newer areas of the garden on a hill, but also there is no road access to the house, which severely limits the use of any heavy materials.

Naila notes: "I don't plan this garden on paper, I'm quite an impulsive and impetuous person, so here I don't feel I have to be professional. I do a

lot of sitting and looking and thinking about what I would change." The garden is used for trialling plants – if they are successful, they can then be used in clients' gardens. Naila's points out that this "works both ways, although it breaks the rules, I do sometimes try something out on clients, then find it works well and use it in my own garden… plants are so incredibly forgiving – you can change things so easily."

"I love my work and at weekends I love my garden. This is my playground, the phone doesn't ring, no-one bothers me. I'm a bit of a hermit, deep down I prefer my own company, my idea of a holiday is two weeks in the garden."

A very personal garden, and one that feels very "undesigned", Naila's densely planted and exuberant vegetation is essentially based on her plant selection skills. She is lucky in having many good plant sources nearby, but it is her enthusiasm for new plants and a willingness to give them a go that has enabled her to achieve this very successful and unusual garden.

A SMALL area of decking sits amidst a mass of planting. The site is exposed to south and west winds – a bank of much taller shrubs helps protect from the colder easterlies. On the seaward side is a hedge of *Rosa rugosa*, a very useful species for barriers – it is a coastal plant it in its native Japan.

Some Favourite Plants

Cistus 'Silver Pink'

Cistus are quintessentially
Mediterranean sub-shrubs, but with a
good enough record in many cooler
climates to be used for ground cover
– for which this variety is particularly
useful. Greyish, evergreen leaves
cover a compact mat of branches –
does not grow above 50cm (19in), but
spreads out to 1m (3ft) wide. Pale
pink flowers in early summer. Sun
essential, tolerant of drought and
poor soils. ZONE 7 MIN.

Gaura lindheimeri

Rangy stems, which seem to go off
in all directions, carry a profusion of
white flowers for several months in
mid- to late summer, making this a
popular, if sometimes difficult to
place, perennial – perhaps best
planted where it can stretch over or
through shorter growing or earlier-
flowering plants – to 1m (3ft) high.
Often short-lived, needs full sun,
good drainage and shelter.
ZONE 5 MIN.

Hebe 'Shiraz'

An uncommon hebe variety that,
according to Naila, forms "lovely
round shapes", with narrow
burgundy-flushed dark green leaves.
The purple flowers appear in late
summer. Wind- and salt-tolerant like
all hebes, moist, but well-drained,
soil. Full sun is important to keep
plants compact – to 80cm (31in) high.
ZONE 8 MIN.

Lysimachia ephemerum

A distinctive, if rather subtle, perennial, with tall (1m/3ft) spires ending in spikes of small off-white flowers and decorated with grey leaves. Its appearance is cool and rather distinguished, a good companion to bright pinks and fresh greens. Naila says, "I use it a lot, but it needs cool moist soil." Likes sun or light shade. ZONE 7 MIN.

Penstemon 'Garnet'

"Penstemons flower for such a long time here, even in December, and this variety is so reliable," says Naila of a hybrid of a colourful, if sometimes short-lived, genus. Scarlet, tubular bells adorn stems that can grow to 80cm (31in). This is quite a compact plant, with a profusion of shoots produced at the base. It dislikes wet winters, so plant in full sun in well-drained soil. Hard pruning at the end of the year will help produce healthy, bushy plants the next year. ZONE 7 MIN.

Phlomis fruticosa Jerusalem sage

Bright yellow flowers adorn a sub-shrub with deep green, felty leaves in early summer. Drought-tolerant, and growing to around 40cm (15½in) high and 80cm (31in) across, it makes a good plant for a hot dry bank. Like lavender, it benefits from a hard prune after flowering to reduce the likelihood of gappy, leggy growth. Full sun, good drainage. ZONE 7 MIN.

Isabelle Greene Santa Barbara, California, USA

KEY TO THE Isabelle Greene design style is unpretentiousness and modesty. These two qualities also stand out in her own garden. Occupying an average-sized lot, the garden is about 700 sq m (9000 sq ft), surrounding a 1948 mail order house, into which Isabelle and her husband John moved in 2005. "I went through the same process as I do with clients," Isabelle explains. "The house has needs, and John and I have needs… the lot is gently sloping upwards, but at the front of the house the land is at grade (flat). We want to stay in the house as we get older, so level ground is important to us." The existing trees, two apricots and a loquat, were left

and the garden designed around them – as is very much her practice.

A vegetable patch, with cloches and wigwams of canes for training climbing beans, adds a homely touch to a garden that, at first sight, clearly belongs to someone who loves plants. The Santa Barbara climate is one of the most rewarding to garden in, allowing many temperate and warm zone species to coexist. There are plenty of familiar perennials here, but succulents, such as species of *crassula* and *echeveria*, as well. The love of stone, which comes across very clearly in Isabelle's design work, is apparent here too, with local stone and left-over broken concrete built up

LOOSELY LAID stone-retaining walls look rustic and without conscious design intent, reflecting the understated look of much of Isabelle's work. Such walls look more grounded if some plants are included which spill over the edges or grow out of cracks.

BIOGRAPHY Unusually for a Californian, Isabelle Greene (1934) is the third generation of her family to live in the state; her grandfather Henry Mather Greene (1870–1954) was a major figure in the Craftsman architectural movement', in California, and also nationally. Isabelle's roots must help to account for her sensitivity to the landscape – she has been practising sustainability for far longer than the word has been fashionable; Isabelle Greene gardens belong in their landscape, and above all they use its precious water responsibly.

Isabelle studied Botany at the University of California and went on to study Landscape Architecture at post-graduate level – a career trajectory that is surprisingly, and perhaps unfortunately, rare. She got her first garden commission in 1964 and steadily built up her portfolio; from the early 1970s, magazine features about her work became frequent and regular. She is one of the very few landscape designers who has been made a fellow by the Society of Landscape Architects.

No other designers I have come across show Isabelle's level of sheer inventiveness – you can visit several of her gardens in quick succession and not believe that they are by the same designer. A variety of well-chosen plants always occupies central place. Rock usually does as well, but in an understated way – it either looks like it is there naturally, or if not, it is intentionally artistic. In the land of conspicuous consumption, hard landscaping is used only where it is needed, never gratuitously. As an alternative, Isabelle has developed the concept of "earthenscape", a sustainable alternative to hard surfacing – for instance, coloured gravels or broken tiles, water-permeable and visually highly effective when combined with ground cover or succulents with interesting, coloured foliage or distinctive texture.

It comes as no surprise to learn that Isabelle sees one of her main influences as being Japanese gardens – their rocks, their relationship to landscape, their

asymmetry. Isabelle describes how she has "always been fascinated by how things looked... I love the shape of the foothills, so sensuous, I try to capture this with shrub shapes." In a state where the marketing of fantasy has become an industry, Isabelle emphasises that we must love the land for what it is. "A great many people want to create a fantasy, of England or Hawaii... but it is a shallow dream which backfires, the real kind of luxury is to make the most of what is there already."

Much garden design in the USA continues to follow a European model – virtually any designer of note has tried to escape this, but a great many others have been unable, or unwilling, to escape the dead hand of European classicism; few have articulated this as clearly as Isabelle: "Classical gardens, with axial paths... it has been done, there's nothing further that can be done with it." In rejecting this model, Isabelle is staying very close to the ideals of the American Arts and Crafts movement of her grandfather – on the American west coast, these architects and designers aimed to produce a style that was true to its materials and owed nothing to European models.

into unmortared retaining walls, a low wall around the vegetable patch, stepping stones, stones around a small pool and the occasional random stone to add personality.

"It was sheer delight purchasing a tear-down house, but saving it and redesigning it for ourselves," recalls Isabelle. "The garden is intensely experimental, including quite a few plants I've never been acquainted with, things I have fallen in love with, planted in ones and twos – this is the antithesis of design, so what I did was to establish a colour theme which has five different levels." Overarching colour schemes are an effective way

of unifying plantings with disparate plant species. The colour scheme was dictated by the view from the bedroom and its colour scheme – there could be no yellow in sight. Grey foliage starts at the edge of the drive, gives way to green, "then around the pond area, which is central to the bedroom view, it's green foliage with blue flowers, then green with pink, then green with orange and yellow beyond the bedroom view."

"I wanted a water feature, for wildlife, but the only place we could put it was atop a wall," says Isabelle, somewhat uneasily, as it is a fundamental rule of naturalistic garden and landscape design

THE VEGETABLE plot, with (left) a loquat tree (*Eriobotrya japonica*) and (right) a small pool, which has been designed to look as natural as possible – an example of an area of a garden acting as a microcosm of a wider world; in this case, streams and pools in the Californian Sierra.

BEARDED IRISES thrive
in California's
Mediterranean climate,
as do almonds (the tree
with the pink flowers).
Iris flowering times are
short, but their foliage
can be relied on to look
good throughout the
growing season.

that bodies of water should be created only in places where they might be expected naturally, "so I think of it as a tarn in the sierra... where I like to go hiking." The very low, ground-covering vegetation around the pool is, according to Isabelle, modelled on "what you find along watercourses in the sierra" – the species used are not natives, but all established horticultural plants: creeping thymes, low-growing varieties of alchemilla, a creeping potentilla, *Arabis alpina*, *Gypsophila nana* and the dwarf mint, *Mentha requenii*. "I'm not a purist about natives," says Isabelle, going on to explain that whether she specifies natives or not depends on the situation: "For clients in the chapparal[2], I use all natives, in case any species get out and cause problems".

2 Chapparal is similar to the maquis of the Mediterranean, a shrubby flora of drought-resistant and fire-resilent shrubs; it is the natural flora of much of California.

"The backyard is like a remembrance from my childhood," says Isabelle. "We have a vegetable garden that produces an enormous amount of food, we give a lot away, we've just tried New Zealand spinach, which was a great success… there are Brussels sprouts 7ft (2m) high that seem to keep on going." The soil has not been easy to work, but Isabelle seems unfazed by it.

She explains: "It's adobe clay, you can't put a spade in it when it's dry, the neighbours hate it, but I put on 6in (15cm) of mulch and let it sit for a year – that helps." Growing vegetables always requires that people work at their soil, but a lifelong philosophy of choosing plants that are appropriate for the place will be sure to stand Isabelle in good stead here too.

Yellow *Bulbine frutescens* (left) flourishes alongside *Crassula ovata* (right) – commonly known as the Jade Plant. Succulents are particularly suitable for areas alongside the foundation of houses, which tend to be in "rain shadow".

Some Favourite Plants All of these are California natives.

Ribes sanguineum 'Spring Showers'

"A beautiful, long-lasting array of pink tassels in the spring, and the foliage holds up for weeks in bouquets," says Isabelle. This is one of many selections from an easy-going shrub that likes sun or light shade. Found wild up the west coast as far as British Columbia, so fine in cool temperate climates – to 2m (6½ft) high. ZONE 6 MIN.

Ceanothus 'Concha'

"Dense deep blue bloom, tidy, compact 'floaty', flat-topped shrub," says Isabelle. A classic, early summer flowering, Californian plant with evergreen foliage clothing a compact-shaped 1.8m (6ft) shrub. Suitable for hot and dry locations; plants are, however, often short-lived on fertile soils and may be damaged by cold winds. ZONE 7 MIN.

Salvia clevelandii 'Allen Chickering'

According to Isabelle, it "blooms practically all year – a hummingbird, bees and bumblebee draw." With aromatic, grey-green foliage, it is drought-tolerant, but like many other Californian/Mexican sages, this variety can be grown as a half-hardy plant in cooler climates, flowering in late summer – to 1.2m (4ft) high. ZONE 8 MIN.

Iris douglasiana

"Spring blooms in bursts of frilly white, to creams, golden yellows, pinks, violets, purples – even mauve and rusty reds," Isabelle notes. This species, along with others in the group known as 'Pacific Coast' iris, is, she stresses, "small and tidy – behaving more like your normal garden plants than many natives" – (60cm/2ft). Light shade and slightly acidic soils preferred. ZONE 7 MIN.

Thalictrum polycarpum

"I use it for its delicate array of slender green stalks clothed with feathery leaves like maidenhair ferns, attenuating to greenish florets," says Isabelle of this plant's subtle beauty, adding that "in autumn the whole plant becomes a translucent gold." Drought tolerant, but prefers shade – to 70cm (30in) high. ZONE 4 MIN.

Erigeron glaucus

"A splendid and tidy ground cover – slowly spreading, to a leafy, even-topped reach of about 1 sq m (8 sq ft), topped for a while in spring with what you must call 'dear posies' – a fringe of tidy, lavender petals surrounding a yellow, central disc" – to 15–30cm (6–12in) high. Highly successful as a seaside plant in Europe as well as California. ZONE 3 MIN.

Penelope Hobhouse Bettiscombe, Dorset, UK

THERE IS SOMETHING of the feeling about Penelope that her garden design career took her by surprise. Any successful career develops its own momentum, and success can pull in directions that were never originally intended. She gained a reputation as "the colour lady", but when she took on the first blank slate of a garden she had ever had, at Bettiscombe in Dorset, she was determined "to do just what I wanted." "People are so obsessed with colour schemes," she says. "Tintinhull exhausted me with them. It felt like I was being imposed upon by an outside force".

When she moved into a converted coach house at Bettiscombe in 1993, Penelope wanted to create a garden that, in its simplicity of form, would encapsulate all that she felt was best about the classical tradition. Whatever the nature of the planting, she believes that effective garden design requires an underlying understanding of forms and masses. At Bettiscombe the plants Penelope used were the evergreen, woody species that had been her first love at Hadspen. They had perhaps become more fashionable since the wave of historically inspired garden design, which Penelope's garden history writing had helped bring about, but they were, however, still very much a minority interest. The comment that "green is so restful" is something that any

LOOKING FROM the gravel garden through Penelope's converted coachouse to the more open area beyond. Notice how plants are sprawling over the gravel path – this is very much the intended effect, the sense of a framework being blurred and softened by planting.

BIOGRAPHY History will probably remember Penelope Hobhouse (born 1929) as a key figure in the garden history movement, and as a writer on a range of garden-related topics. Driven by an insatiable intellectual curiosity, scholarly discipline and a self-critical streak, Penelope's varied career has led her from enthusiasm to enthusiasm in the world of gardening – so design has just been one strand amongst many.

Penelope's career as a garden designer began in 1985, following publication of *Colour in your Garden*, the first serious study of this vital design topic for many years. "My working life took off," she says, "people began to contact me, saying things like 'I want a garden like on page 67.' Many of the clients were in the United States, leading her to establish close working relationships with colleagues there, and an increasing workload of lecturing, writing and even an American television series, *The Art and Practice of Gardening* (1996). By the end of the 1990s, the reality of running a major design business in your seventies, much of it on the other side of the Atlantic, began to seem less attractive and she recalls, "your life moves on... I am really a practical gardener." In fact, another great intellectual passion had begun to take over – the gardens of the Islamic world.

"Until I went to Iran, I thought all gardening began in the Renaissance. Now I know it began in central Asia," says Penelope, recalling how Islamic gardens with their strict perpendicular geometry began with a pre-Islamic Persian model. A book on Persian gardens (*The Gardens of Persia*) followed in 2004 and she began to lead garden tours to Iran, as well as to India and Pakistan – the Indian sub-continent having been heavily influenced by Persian civilization.

It was at Hadspen House in Somerset, the home of her first husband's family, where Penelope started gardening; evergreen shrubs were an early interest, encouraged by donations of cuttings from the great garden of Abbotsbury in Dorset, where the Head Gardener had become a friend. From 1979 to 1993 she was a tenant of the National Trust at Tintinhull, living with her second husband, John Malins, a retired professor of medicine, who she remembers as "an enthusiastic and immensely knowledgeable gardener." Phyllis Reiss created Tintinhull's garden, following the colour planting philosophy of Gertrude Jekyll (1843–1932). "It was my first experience of a

perennial garden," she recalls. "We stuck to all Mrs. Reiss's colour schemes, but we wanted to experiment with different plants, although the National Trust didn't like us changing anything, and we had to plant things behind their backs." It was at Tintinhull that Penelope developed her design philosophy that can be summed up as "create a grid and then let it become a jungle as soon as possible." One highlight of Penelope's life at Tintinhull was the programme she recorded with Audrey Hepburn for a series called *Gardens of the World*.

Whilst Penelope's career as writer and designer was taking off elsewhere, others were establishing their careers at Hadspen, which, during the 1990s, gained a reputation for sophisticated colour scheming. Nori and Sandra Pope managed the garden from 1987 to 2005; they built on the framework of Penelope's planting, and developed a colour scheming system of their own, which received a great deal of praise and attention.

GARDENS OPEN TO THE PUBLIC

- **The Walled Garden** at Aberglasney House, Carmarthenshire, Wales

- **The Queen Mother's garden** at Walmer Castle, Kent, UK

- **The Luce Herb garden** at the New York Botanical Garden, USA

- **The Isiah Davenport House** Savannah, Georgia, USA

- **The Summer garden** at The Royal Horticultural Society Garden, Wisley, UK

gardener would agree with, but few would act on with the conviction that Penelope did. "But," she hastily adds, "I'm not anti-flower."

Penelope's home at Bettiscombe was a converted coach house. The garden that she set

to work on was a 1,600 sq m (0.4 acre) walled kitchen garden, with "the walls in a bad state of repair, and all the worst weeds: Japanese knotweed, ground elder and horsetail; I didn't keep anything." There was a "slope across the line

of vision from the house, so I changed the levels… the soil was terrible, waterlogged clay, almost unworkable, so I imported lots of topsoil and put in drainage." Traditionally, fit young men would double dig such soil, with manure dug into the soil to the depths of two spits[1]. "But you can't find anyone to double dig anymore, so I had one bed along a wall rotovated, which was a mistake as it made a hardpan, making drainage even worse," she remembers. The garden was 100m (328ft) above sea level, but "south-facing, so I avoided the very worst frosts, and I could grow all my favourite evergreens"; it was also near enough the south coast (7.5km/4½ miles) that mild temperatures prevailed. The wet soil, however, meant that much herbaceous planting was done in raised beds that offered better drainage.

The walled garden is a near perfect example of Penelope's expression of her garden design philosophy, of framework filled in with jungle.

Axial paths provide bones, along with low box hedges and pollarded *Robinia pseudoacacia* 'Umbraculifera' – a rounded form of a widely planted tree. A scramble of perennials and low Mediterranean shrubs amply covers these bones. In fact, much of this is a gravel garden, originally laid out for *The Art and Practice of Gardening*. This area had been a lawn, but it became so dry during the summer that a more water-wise replacement seemed a good idea. "Most of the plants I chose were self-seeders," says Penelope, the idea being that gravel gardens provide a good home for species that spread themselves through seeding, but which also make it possible to pull out weeds or unwanted seedlings easily. As the gravel garden became established, it became more and more exuberant, with a particularly wide range of foliage shapes and textures: majestic, large, silvery-leaved globe artichokes (*Cynara cardunculus*), low-sprawling sage (*Salvia*

THE SOFT yellow of Tree Lupin (*Lupinus arboreus*) (rear, right) is echoed by the gold of *Phlomis fruticosa* (front, centre). Clipped standard *Robinia pseudoacacia* 'Umbraculifera' (rear, right) contribute 'backbone'. Straight axial paths are important too for structure.

officinalis) and *Alchemilla mollis*, small rounded shrubs such as *Phlomis fruticosa*, grasses such as *Stipa gigantea* and thrusting spires – *Verbascum* species in flower and seed. There was never a shortage of colour, mostly yellows and purples, but plenty of pinks too, particularly from roses, some of which were trained on arches, so adding a dash of English romanticism.

Self-seeding is inherently unpredictable, but is most likely with biennials or short-lived perennials – very often these are species with larger than average seeds that germinate well in gravel. The dramatic thistle-like *Eryngium giganteum*, and the subtle greeny yellow flowered *Bupleurum falcatum*, soon began to spread here. Both are members of the *Apiaceae*[2]; another member is the particularly dramatic *Ferula communis*, the giant fennel with yellow flower heads atop 3m (10ft) high stems.

"Over time," Penelope notes, "I got less and less interested in flowers, so they gradually got eliminated. It got to the point that if I spent the day in the gravel garden I would end up feeling exhausted by the colour, but I kept the roses going." As an antidote, however, she had been developing another part of her property. "At first I didn't think I'd do anything outside the walled garden," she recalls, but once the walled garden began to take shape, Penelope took on planting and shaping more garden out of an acre (4046 sq m) of land on the other side of the house. Here, there were views out to the hills and hedge-bounded fields of the surrounding countryside. Hedges in the garden echo the hedges in the landscape, whilst areas of long meadow grass and bulbs (daffodils and *camassias*) create a further link with the surroundings. From big windows in the house (filling in what would once have been the arch of the coach house door), a vista stretches down an avenue of yew cones at the edge of a wide mown path, backed by meadow grass, to a red painted bench. Two alleys, formed by hedges of hornbeam, stand at right angles to the axial path, and just before the bench is a long narrow formal pool with steel coping, also at right angles to the axis, but scarcely visible from the house. Penelope explains,

2 This is the plant family that used to be known as the *Umbelliferae*, characterized by its "umbels" – plate- or dome-shaped heads of minute flowers, white in most species.

ONE ADVANTAGE of an old coachhouse are large windows. Here a wide path of grass, defined by an alley of yew pyramids and surrounded by meadow, leads the eye out over the distant hills of the Somerset-Dorset border country.

WILDFLOWER MEADOW, grading into rough grass, can always be made to look intentional by formal features. Here a simple, even austere, formal pool reflects the sky and emphasises that this is a designed landscape.

"I felt the area needed more light, which the reflection from water can provide." The atmosphere is distinctly contemporary, restful and outward looking, in contrast to the intimacy and intensity of the walled garden.

Hornbeam (*Carpinus betulus*) was the chosen material for some of hedges – the tree does well in cold wet soil – but, unconventionally, Penelope also used alder for the hedge that stands right at the very back, behind the bench; the tree is one of the best for very wet soils, but so fast-growing that it needs cutting three times a year. In this area, Penelope also planted several wing-nuts (*Pterocarya* species), rapid-growing and expansively elegant relatives of the walnut that Penelope assures us "never mind having their feet in water." The yew chosen for the avenue, however, was not so successful; it is a tree that hates waterlogged soil, so drainage pipes had to be laid at their roots.

In 2008, Penelope retired to a house in the grounds at Hadspen, now owned by her son Niall. Her new garden, although small and intimate, is built around the perpendicular geometry that is at the core of the western garden tradition – although, as she is keen to tell us, "western" here is a very relative term.

On the difference between designing for clients and garden-making for oneself, Penelope notes, "You can do much more in your own garden, there is a freedom; clients would always look after a garden in a very different way." There is sometimes a certain tension in the client-designer relationship, too, as a client can visit your garden or see a picture and say, 'I want this', but you couldn't give it to them." At the end of an illustrious career, most of us would probably agree that Penelope Hobhouse has surely earned the right to say "no".

Some Favourite Plants

Bupleurum fruticosum

A mound-forming (3 x 2m/10 x 6 ½ft) shrub with rounded, glossy, dark evergreen leaves. Small yellow flower heads cover the plant over many weeks in summer. Full sun necessary for the expression of the dense mounded growth that is its charm. Ideal for coastal locations.
ZONE 7 MIN.

Buxus balearica

A box species from Spain and North Africa with large (4 x 2cm/1 ½ x ¾in) bright green leaves, eventually forming a tree 9m (30ft) high with an upright habit. Its large leaves and loose habit make it unsuitable for conventional topiary or hedging, but instead an interesting plant in its own right. Sun or light shade.
ZONE 8 MIN.

Euphorbia mellifera

One of the most magnificent, medium-sized shrubs for foliage – effectively evergreen, although not strictly so, as the elegant, narrow leaves, with their prominent, yellow midribs, generally only last a year. Strongly honey-scented flowers in early summer and a neat rounded habit make this a highly desirable plant. Generally, grows to 2 x 2m (¾ x ¾in) in cultivation, but potentially taller in sheltered locations. Intolerant of cold winds.
ZONE 8 MIN.

Magnolia grandiflora 'Little Gem'

Eventually forming a large tree (10m/ 33ft high), this evergreen with large slightly yellow-flushed glossy green leaves is familiar in many areas with warm temperate or Mediterranean climates, although there is a great tradition of growing it as a wall-shrub in cooler regions. The flowers, borne in summer, are huge, creamy-white and exotically fragrant, but often sparsely produced. This form has smaller leaves and flowers at a younger age than the standard species. ZONE 6 MIN.

Phillyrea latifolia

A classic, Mediterranean shrub that was popular in formal 17th- and 18th-century English gardens. Narrow, darkly evergreen leaves, and a dense branching habit, can make the plant look a little like its less hardy relative, the olive; this is also a good plant to cut into formal shapes – to 3m (10ft) high and wide. Good in coastal gardens. ZONE 7 MIN.

Viburnum x *hillieri* 'Winton'

An evergreen shrub with narrow leaves that are toned red in spring, and sometimes again in autumn and winter. Heads of white flowers in summer lead on to red, and then black fruit – to 2.5m (8ft) high and wide. ZONE 7 MIN.

Raymond Jungles Personal gardens, Florida, USA

URING MY LIFE, I have done four projects for myself," says Raymond, referring to gardens made for homes or studios… "but haven't had my own garden for a while, although I've recently remarried, after a divorce eight years ago, and I'm looking forward to starting a new one." His first garden was made with his former wife Debra Yates, who was a painter, and made ceramic panels that could be permanent features in the garden. One such panel extended out of the house onto the wall of the design studio (which had been converted from a garage) – an innovative idea, emphasising how the Florida climate makes it simple to blur the boundary between indoors and out. In this climate it is easy to say, "I like having breakfast outside in the garden, and then getting up and sculpting a tree."

Raymond and Debra had a garden in Miami from 1987 to 1995 on a 1,000 sq m (10,764 sq ft) plot. "We wanted to create privacy using the most economical means possible", says Raymond. This they achieved by re-locating the "foundation planting"[1] from around the house to borders along the boundaries, and by building a fence around the property and painting it black – this was largely concealed by the planting (which was almost entirely evergreen), but had the effect of creating a sense of depth.

THE ROSETTE of large leaves is a common feature of tropical foliage. Here the shapes of a bromeliad (foreground), a cycad (centre foreground) and palms echo each other. The climber *Ficus pumila* coats the wall next to the door.

BIOGRAPHY Florida is unique in the continental United States in having a sub-tropical climate, so the demands on plants, the range of native species and the visual aesthetics are completely different to those in any other American state, which rather puts Raymond Jungles in a special position. "I work a lot in the Caribbean," he says; his perspective is inevitably outwards and southwards, especially towards Brazil, a country with which he has a very special link. "I knew Roberto Burle Marx well," he recalls. "I stayed with him every year for fourteen years... he became my mentor... I sold his paintings, although I never did any landscape design with him. I'd travel around with him and become part of his entourage. He'd let me take cuttings from anything, I still use a lot of those plants."

Born in Omaha, Nebraska (in 1956), Raymond became interested in landscape design after moving to Florida in 1974; it was while he was at the University of Florida, studying landscape architecture, that he went to a lecture by Burle Marx – the two got talking and the rest, as they say, is history.

The Jungles practice is largely concerned with making private gardens, but they have also been involved with the landscape design of corporate and civic spaces. Raymond has also designed an orchid display at the New York Botanical Garden (2009); the modernist arrangement of structures and plants was a tribute to Burle Marx.

GARDENS OPEN TO THE PUBLIC

- **Plaza** at 1111, Lincoln Road, Miami Beach, Florida, USA (under construction)

- **New World Symphony Centre** Miami Beach, Florida, USA (under construction)

- **The Brazilian Garden** at the Naples Botanic Garden, Naples, Florida, USA

- **Master plan for the Key West Botanical Garden** Key West, Florida, USA

- **Golden Rock Inn** Nevis, West Indies

A number of structures were built for Raymond and Debra's children (Benjamin and Amanda), including a tree-house perched on a defunct radio antenna. Raymond explains, "I design for children in the same way I design for adults, as I think kids react to things in the same way adults do, I'm a kid myself. Mystery and wonder are important for children, butterflies, birds and wildlife are very important, ponds for fish and turtles, kids love anything alive." Amanda recalls "growing up on job sites... with my brother I'd be in the garden all day. I remember things like finding frogs in the bromeliads by flashlight." She probably won't become a landscape architect, but the beauty of

1 "Foundation planting" refers to evergreen shrubs planted at the base of the house wall. Its use is very widespread in the United States, but is often criticised by gardeners as unimaginative and stereotypical.

INSPIRED BY Mexican architect Luis Barragan, this red wall is a good complement to the dark green which can be so overwhelming in the tropics. Its colour is picked up by a *Codiaeum* cultivar in the foreground.

the gardens she grew up in has inspired her artistic side – "I'm a poet, I do it through words," she adds. Benjamin, meanwhile, has been directly influenced by his dad's work, and is studying interior design.

In 1997, Raymond designed a garden for Debra's mother, Eva, in Key West; after she died, he and Debra lived there for a number of years. A square plot, with an almost centrally positioned house, and a studio and swimming pool occupying much of the rest of the 950 sq m (10,225 sq ft) space, resulted in garden areas being restricted to the edges and intervening spaces – a common situation in American gardens. Raymond, however, succeeded in creating a lushly intimate atmosphere, where planting enclosed small areas of terracing. Surrounding trees cast heavy shade, so the planting had to be shade-tolerant – rainforest floor species were particularly useful. In fact, much of the planting was with Brazilian material – "Roberto used to give me plants, and I had an area where I grew them, to see how they did. The best I would pass on to nurseries to propagate." Luis Barragan-style painted walls, on which plants in the garden cast a constantly moving pattern of shadow, played an important role in screening and in breaking up space.

"I'm a frustrated sculptor," says Raymond. "In a garden I want to express some of my sculptural tendencies." A private garden is the ideal place to work out new approaches to planting design, and try out new materials – all the more important for someone working with sub-tropicals, which in many ways is still an area for pioneers.

Florida presents the designer with many challenges, both on the environmental front and in design terms. Much of the soil is very alkaline, with a very low organic matter content (which restricts the ability of the soil to hold water and

nutrient reserves) and it has a prolonged dry season. It is also very flat – so there are rarely any views or elevations that can be included in designs. As a consequence, gardens need to be visually "self-sufficient".

"I believe gardens should provide habitat for the wildlife that used to live here," says Raymond, recalling the range of rich, natural habitats that, until relatively recently, covered much of the state. "I have always been an ecologist at heart," he says, "which was reinforced by knowing Roberto, and how he used Brazilian natives… over the years I believe I have had a lot of influence on the use of natives here." Certainly, the increase in legislation that mandates a fixed percentage of native plants in new developments has forced many in the landscape business to

pay more attention to what they plant. Raymond's planting often conveys a sense of wildness that is just under control, in contrast to that of many other designers who work with tropical plants, and find it all too easy to rely on the intrinsic foliage drama of warm-climate plants. He likes boundaries to give "a sense of the woods, so that gardens feel like clearings", while the use of signature natives like the sabal palm (*Sabal palmetto*) "look like they have always been there." He is also fond of "fragmented paving", whereby paving stones are laid with gaps between them wide enough for ribbons of grass to grow – the effect is to soften the impact of the hard surface and to subtly remind us that nature could one day swallow up everything we have built.

Children's play areas need to be as open to interpretation or multiple-use as possible, especially in smaller gardens. Built structures in particular can provide opportunities for both physical and imaginative play, and can often be adapted to changing uses as children get older.

THE BLUE OF a pool is repeated in furnishings and a ceramic painting by Debra Yates. The scale of some of the trees here helps convey the poetic conceit that this might be an isolated retreat in the forest, as well as providing all important shade.

Some Favourite Plants

Coccoloba diversifolia Pigeon Plum

Potentially a tree to 10m (33ft) high, this leathery-leaved species is often smaller in cultivation or in colder or windier climates. Branching is upright, and the resulting neat habit has made it popular with landscapers. Spring sees the plant covered in spikes of white flowers, which are followed by dark purple berries – a great wildlife resource. Salt- and drought-tolerant. ZONE 10 MIN.

Leucothrinax morrisii Brittle Thatch Palm

One of the classic palms of the Caribbean and the Florida Keys, this fan-leaved species grows to around 10m (33ft) high. Its common name indicates an important traditional use. It needs full sun; is relatively drought-, wind- and salt-tolerant, once established. Easy to grow. ZONE 10 MIN.

Myrcianthes fragrans Twinberry, Simpson's Stopper

Small, dark green leaves, heavily aromatic with a nutmeg type scent, make for an attractive shrub or small tree for coastal gardens in warm climates. Growing to a maximum of 10m (33ft), it can be kept smaller through pruning or clipping. Fragrant white flowers are produced over a long season, leading to edible red fruit, which are also much appreciated by birdlife. Tolerant of a wide range of soils, drought, and some shade. ZONE 9 MIN.

Quercus virginiana Southern Live Oak

"Live" refers to the evergreen foliage of this magnificent tree, a vital part of the landscape of the American South. Its branches are also the favoured home of Spanish moss – the grey bromeliad that is so typical of the South. Eventually forming a tree growing to 20m (65ft) high and wide, this is not something for the small garden, but for larger gardens the cultivation of young live oaks will ensure heritage landscapes for future generations. Best in deep soils. ZONE 10 MIN.

Sabal palmetto Cabbage palm or palmetto

A robust palm with a head of dull green leaves that, from a distance, has a light feathery look – but does not look like a cabbage! The old leaf bases tend to persist on the trunk, so developing a criss-cross pattern. Usually reaches a height of 15m (49ft), but may exceed this. The leaves are around 3.5m (11ft) long, tend to be longer in shade, and are intermediate in form – not clearly pinnate or palmate (fan-shaped). Tolerates light shade, standing water, and light frosts. ZONE 8 MIN.

Serenoa repens Saw Palmetto

A "shrubby" palm, with multiple stems emerging from the base to a height of 3m (10ft). Palmate leaves can grow to 3m (10ft) wide. With time a wide mass of growth is formed – so considerable space is needed, plus a wide enough landscape for the plant not to dominate its surroundings. Some forms have attractive silvery or bluish tinged foliage. Tolerant of shade, and, once established, drought and frosts. ZONE 7 MIN.

Jantiene T. Klein Roseboom The Roof Garden, Amsterdam, Netherlands

ANTIENE DESCRIBES a 55 sq m (592 sq ft) roof garden she made when she lived in central Amsterdam in the 1980s as being "a formative experience, the first garden I designed myself." The garden is situated on the roof of a 17th-century merchant's house situated on one of Amsterdam's historic canals. She had employed a "leading local garden designer" to design a garden for the roof of her house, but she was not happy with the plans. She says they were "entirely based on constraints, not possibilities, so in the end I designed it myself, working with a structural engineer to specify a purpose-built steel structure so that the roof could take the weight which

allowed for a real garden." Although she still owns the property, it is Jantiene's tenants who now enjoy the views from the roof garden, which includes the distinctive profile of the city's Rijksmuseum. Wooden planters 60cm (2ft) deep provide enough root space for a beech hedge, which helps to provide at least some shelter from what Jantiene describes as "the constant wind you get in Amsterdam."

"Everything in there is hardy," says Jantiene, "apart from a few annuals which I change every year." Summer-flowering annuals, which at least have to endure only the less windy part of the year, play a crucial role in bringing a softer look

A ROOF garden has to be a place which is extra-ordinary, at the same time rooted in a down-to-earth normality; features like brick walls are an important part of this "grounding". Plants growing below them will be sheltered from the worst winds.

BIOGRAPHY Jantiene T. Klein Roseboom (born 1961) is one of those who have made a dramatic career change – in this case from working in capital markets for more than twenty years. Jantiene recalls how she once discovered a childhood scrapbook – in it were rare wild flowers, carefully dried, arranged and labelled, and plans of gardens. It was something she had completely forgotten about, but it indicates that from a very early age she had been fascinated by nature and by gardens. She considered landscape architecture at university, but ended up studying economics instead. This led to further study at Harvard Business School, and London Business School, and a career specializing in strategy, finance and mergers, and acquisitions.

Childhood trips to the Alps had made Jantiene especially aware of the beauty of plant communities, the development of which she regards as a particularly important part of her design work, which is heavily weighted towards naturalistic plant combinations set within clearly structured frameworks. Another early influence was Piet Oudolf. Jantiene says "My parents had known of his work and bought plants from his nursery many years before he became well-known" (they lived near Hummelo, where the Oudolfs moved to in 1981), so she feels "that I grew up with his style of plant." From an early age she was also taught by her father how to look at and consider the context of wider landscapes – he was considered a leading figure in countryside management and the successful reconciliation of agricultural, (socio) economic and ecological interests; he even received a government award for this work.

Jantiene's career in international finance was, needless to say, extremely demanding, and inevitably involved a lot of travel. However, unlike many in this world who go straight from airport to hotel room to conference suite, she would grab some time out whenever she could – even if only minutes – and get a sense of local landscape and horticulture. Dealing with financial assets professionally, and drawing on her early landscape lessons from her father, she began to feel that

"landscape is actually the most precious asset we have – the value of which is immeasurable." And so began the germ of the idea of a new career, although it took many years before this materialised.

Now firmly settled in England, she gained a post-graduate degree in residential landscape architecture at Oxford in 2006, and "a lot of globally conducted self-study" gave Jantiene the confidence to start a new profession. "Because of my business background," she says, "I'm used to working at the higher end of the market... I'm used to handling large and complex projects, and adopting a multi-disciplinary approach... I also like to work on longer-running schemes which develop over time..." An important part of her approach is to consider "the place of the garden in its landscape... this is not necessarily something a client thinks about immediately." Jantiene continues, "so when I take on a garden, I will research a wide-ranging area surrounding it, and elements of the wider landscape are always echoed in the garden, resulting in a sense of belonging and serenity."

to the rooftop environment. Plants selected for roof gardens need to be physically resilient, to cope with the buffeting from wind, and preferably drought-tolerant – at least, if the automatic irrigation system that Jantiene regards as "absolutely essential" is not used. An interesting point she raises is that "irrigation is especially crucial in early spring, when hedges are coming into leaf." She also recommends planting densely, so that plants can help to support each other

(as does Naila Green in her coastal garden). Jantiene also recommends including some wild flower species, such as wild carrot (*Daucus carota*), for their toughness as well as helping create a relaxed look.

Surprisingly, Jantiene noticed that wildlife take as much advantage of a rooftop garden as a ground-level one, even frogs and newts – and a duck came to nest one year! "Nature," she says, "always prevails – as it should."

Roof gardens can be exposed, both to sun and wind. Jantiene's answer was the construction of a pergola type framework that could be used to support a canvas awning when the roof was being actively used. Notice the decking – a lightweight construction technique particularly useful for use on roofs.

Some Favourite Plants

Carpinus betulus

Hornbeam has long been used as a hedging tree, but is still somewhat underrated. Similar in appearance to beech, but growing much better on cold wet soils, or at northern latitudes. It can be cut and shaped into thinner hedge, with a finer line than beech, enabling the adventurous to clip a variety of interesting effects. ZONE 5 MIN.

Craetegus laevigata

Hawthorns are very good shrubs or small trees for exposed places, and they grow fast and develop densely twiggy growth – ideal for clipping, but given that they are so fast, this needs to be done frequently, several times every summer. White or pink flowers in spring – depending on variety, although flower production on clipped plants will be reduced. ZONE 5 MIN.

Digitalis ferruginea

This foxglove relative has narrowly elegant and tall (to 1.4m/4 ¾ft) flower stems, densely packed with intricately marked flowers in various shades of fawn and brown. As seed heads, they are sturdily spectacular through the winter if the plant is grown en masse. Short-lived but often self-sows to form dramatic clumps. ZONE 7 MIN.

Erigeron karvinskianus

"Prolifically self-seeding, carving out a place in the most hostile environments. Allow it to interweave itself through grasses, in between paving and along edges to create a natural look," Jantiene notes. This little (to 20cm/8in) daisy relative is perhaps most widely appreciated as self-seeding into the stone steps of many a traditional English garden. Short-lived and not very hardy, but given its seed production, this is rarely a problem. ZONE 8 MIN.

Knautia macedonica

The deep red flowers of this perennial are useful for dotting in and around clumps of paler-flowered plants, when the rather gangly stems and generally untidy habit may be hidden. If happy, it will flower for months – to 80cm (31in). Likes full sun and any soil. Limited lifespan but readily self-seeds. ZONE 5 MIN.

Perovskia atriplicifolia "Blue Spire"

One of the most useful plants for mid-summer colour, this is a perennial from semi-desert areas across Asia – and so is ideal for hot, dry situations, along with alkaline soils and the coast. The dead flower stems have a white bloom that gives it a certain amount of winter interest – to 1m (3ft) high. ZONE 3 MIN.

Arabella Lennox-Boyd Gresgarth Hall, Lancashire, UK

THE GARDEN at Gresgarth Hall was one of the bigger surprises of my writing this book. I had Arabella down as a Designer, with a capital "D", and had not realised the extent to which she is first and foremost a gardener, with the love of plant-collecting typical of gardeners in her adopted homeland. The garden here is a veritable treasure trove of both the familiar and the unfamiliar. Trees are a particular interest, but so are old roses, unusual shrubs, moisture-loving perennials, and rhododendrons – and there is a lush and lovingly tended kitchen garden. "Gardening is my total passion," she says.

Arabella and Mark Lennox-Boyd moved in to Gresgarth in 1979, and started work on the garden in 1981. The "gardened" area now extends to 9 acres (3½ hectares), with three gardeners. "I spend every moment I can steal from office work in the garden," says Arabella, "usually at weekends, and sometimes I manage to spend a whole week at Gresgarth. I do nearly all the propagation, and then all the potting up. I love making my own compost and experimenting with different ones. I place the plants that need to be planted, and plan borders and plants that I wish to try out. You may think I am eccentric, but I adore weeding and making a bed look just so. I have a

A VIEW FROM the upper storey of the house – a quintessentially English combination of roses, clipped box and herbaceous plants. An arboretum is developing on the other side of the beck (river).

BIOGRAPHY Arabella, Lady Lennox-Boyd (born 1938) heads a design company that has established a reputation as one of the world's most prestigious, designing gardens and landscapes for both private and corporate clients. The company has worked in a number of different countries, some very disparate climate zones, and on every scale, from large estates to roof gardens to cramped urban spaces. Clients have included the Duke of Westminster, Sir Terence Conran and the musician Sting.

Arabella originally studied landscape design at Thames Polytechnic just at the time when the profession of garden designer was becoming seen as a discipline in its own right. A succession of Chelsea Flower Show gardens (with six gold medals to date) illustrates the wide range of design approaches the practice takes. "I don't have a style," says Arabella, "a garden has to be made for individual owners... I try to understand the hopes and feelings of my clients, how they are going to live in and use the garden, I try to see what they want from it, I try to give shape and meaning to places... I really like sensations, such as the sound of water, the contrast between coolness and light." Two things do, however, dominate the Lennox-Boyd practice's work: the strong structures of European classicism and the plant- and flower-rich legacy of the English, cottage-garden tradition.

Born in Italy, Arabella was brought up in Rome, but spent holidays at a family property, Palazzo Parisi, high in the hills above the city, where she was surrounded by the sights and smells of rural Italy. Although she still owns it, she spends nearly all her time in London, or at home at Gresgarth Hall, Lancashire. "I have to go to Italy for a week every year to see my tree peonies and for other brief visits, but otherwise I entirely garden at Gresgarth," she says. A very English gardener she may be, but Arabella's strong sense of design is something she sees as being in her Italian roots.

meeting once a week on a Saturday with the Head Gardener and we discuss the programme."

"When we came," says Arabella, "there was no garden, but a lot of trees, it was a 19th-century mini-romantic landscape... we felt uncomfortable with the house on a slope, so we built a terrace in the late 1980s." She went on to explain, "I did not design the garden, it evolved." Although there had been no ornamental gardening in her family, "Mark's mother had been a famous gardener in Cornwall[1]. She propagated and grew all the box for us, and gave us lots of other plants."

Essentially Victorian, the house has high gothic-inspired windows and a modest tower, and sits in a shallow amphitheatre, open to the west. The view south from the terrace is of a 180° sweep of trees – broadleaved woodland as a backdrop to a legacy of classic 19th-century planting (mature beeches and evergreens such as the immense wellingtonia, *Sequioadendron giganteum*) and younger trees of Arabella's planting; the range of shapes and foliage textures shown by the trees is remarkable. The garden visible from here is centred around a small lake, but if you walk to one side, an energetically moving river (the Artle Beck) is revealed, with a Chinese-style bridge leading to another whole area that Arabella is developing as an arboretum. Trees and shrubs have been sought from the small nurserymen who specialise in rarer plants, but recently Arabella has been growing young plants on from seed collected on expeditions to China and Japan – in doing so, she is following a long-established tradition whereby owners of large country gardens support plant hunters and new plant introductions.

Horticultural riches are largely hidden from this first view from the terrace; instead what dominates is a steep grassy bank on the far side of the river, topped and surrounded by trees – a good example of a "borrowed landscape", it brings a wilder environment right into the garden. "One

1 At Ince Castle, near Plymouth, in Cornwall.

OVERLOOKED by a single
flower of *Meconopsis
betonicifolia*, a pool is
fronted by the dramatic
flowerheads of *Darmera
peltata* into which has grown
the wild garlic *Allium
ursinum*. The *Darmera* is very
useful for stabilising muddy
banks. The flowers are
followed by very large
circular leaves.

2 *Rhododendron ponticum*: a species introduced into Britain in the 19th century (although possibly native in the past) and which has become something of an invasive alien in some areas.

3 Mrs. Underwood grew and publicised many of the silver-leaved plants that we take for granted, at a time when they were little known or appreciated. She was a formidable character.

A SERIES of different spaces provide a cornucopia of habitats for a major plant collection. Developments happen against a backdrop of classic nineteenth-century tree planting.

of the first things we did was to clear this slope, it was covered in sycamore and ponticum[2]," says Arabella. Other early major tasks were to extend the lake and install drainage in many of the borders – none of this has been easy, given that the garden is an old river bed, full of stones.

The site has not been an easy one. It is a frost pocket, exposed to westerly winds, funnelled by the valley sides that give the location so much of its character. Rainfall is high while drainage is poor. Arabella admits to having initially felt daunted by the conditions and early failures; she remembers talking to a famously redoubtable nursery owner (Mrs. Underwood) at a Royal Horticultural Society show in the early days, about her despair at an inability to grow any silver-leaved plants[3]. Improving the drainage was advised (as well as showing a bit more stiff upper lip, I think) – it worked, and from then on Arabella "went at planting like a bull in a China shop." Lush, healthy plants are such a feature of this garden – the reason for the lushness is, perhaps, that Arabella has clearly developed a strong sense of what works and what does not. Many ornamental grasses and sun-loving perennials do not thrive, or grow slowly or get wind-damaged, so are not pursued. Any plant that does flourish is repeated, and close relatives tried. "Repetition and rhythm are very important in design," she says; it makes sense to make a point of repeating plants that grow well naturally.

Whilst Gresgarth is first and foremost a very personal garden, it does play an important part in the design business. "I do bring potential clients here," Arabella says, "and trialling is very important, I keep lists and everything is catalogued, most of my knowledge of trees, shrubs and perennials come from here… I learn about how they grow and how they can be maintained… I now provide maintenance documents for clients." Plants, for this practice, are absolutely central, and this exceptionally diverse garden clearly plays a big role in its ongoing success.

A<small>T FIRST</small> sight a classic large herbaceous border, but one with some more contemporary elements, notably the grass *Calamagrostis brachytricha*, which is used here as a very effective rhythmical element. In late summer, a variety of phlox and aster species provide colour.

Some Favourite Plants

Agapanthus

With rich blue, dense flower clusters, carried clear of their straplike leaves, agapanthus are well-established as summer-flowering bulbous plants. Traditionally seen as tender, they can, however, live for many years if planted in situations protected from the worst of the winter. Best left undisturbed, they form dense clumps over time. In warm climates they can be used as ground cover in shade; in cooler ones, they need full sun in a sheltered spot. Good drainage is vital. ZONE 7/8 MIN.

Ampelodesmos mauritanicus

An expansive and majestic grass for large gardens; "unbelievable in Italy, where it will grow in completely dry places," notes Arabella. Fawn flower/ seed heads are thrust out from large tussocks – 3m (10ft) high and across. Full sun. ZONE 8 MIN.

Asphodoline lutea

Despite being a plant from dry, rocky slopes, this perennial self-sows enthusiastically in Gresgarth's moist soil. Narrow 60-cm (24-in) tall spikes of rich yellow above a tuft of narrow leaves in early summer give way to spherical seed heads. Any well-drained soil in sun, but particularly suitable for drought-prone sites or poor stony soils. Best grown in diffuse groups, as the repetition of its yellow spires makes a striking impact. ZONE 6 MIN.

Daphhne bholua

The fact that the scent of this evergreen, upright-growing shrub can spread a considerable distance, and that its flowering season lasts over several months from late winter to early spring, makes it an immensely valuable garden plant. The flower colour varies from pure white to mid-pink – to 2.5m (8ft) in height, and well-drained, but moist soils, and shelter are essential. Like all daphnes, it is relatively short-lived. ZONE 7 MIN.

Nepeta grandiflora 'Bramdean'

"It can be a metre high, but not need staking... looks best behind a lower plant... I like the way the flowers still look good after they have finished," says Arabella, of this large, generally upright catmint relative, with mauve flowers in early to mid-summer and attractive dark stems. Any well-drained soil in sun. ZONE 4 MIN.

Roses

Not wanting to be pinned down on a favourite variety, Arabella mentions the Hybrid Musks as a favourite group of roses, despite their lack of scent; the heavily fragrant Gallicas are also favourites and include many beautiful, historic varieties. The Portland roses, being compact growers, with long or repeat flowering, are especially suitable for small gardens; 'Rose de Rescht', with rich, purple-pink flowers, fragrant and densely packed with petals, is one of the best. ZONE 4 MIN.

Katie Lukas The garden at Stone House, Gloucestershire, UK

I GET ALL MY WORK through word of mouth," says Katie. "The garden is open to the public, and it is a shop window, but not intentionally so… Troubleshooting is often how I start… I love to reclaim gardens, to pull them together."

Katie's own gardening experience was initially gained in London, then Derbyshire and Aberdeenshire. She has been making her current garden in the Cotswolds since 1991, and in the last ten years with her husband Andrew; 2.5 acres (1.1 hectares) of acid clay around a house built of the stone for which the area is famous. Managing it is part of the continual learning process that Katie emphasises is at the very heart both of

gardening and her career. It is open to the public on a regular basis, and attracts a steady stream of coach parties of enthusiastic garden clubs; more than the admission fee changes hands, for Katie says, "I learn something from every group which visits."

Stone House might be many people's idea of a classic English garden, with hedges and walls dividing off one part from another, roses and climbers spilling down from walls and arches, brick paths and clipped box bushes. A stream flows down one side, with lush informal planting along its banks. Views out are encouraged, through having paths that lead the eye towards

A HEDGE of widely spaced *Carpinus betulus* 'Fastigiata' provides an architectural backdrop to the more intensely managed part of Katie's garden. Beyond is an area of meadow grass and trees. The pale yellow (left) is *Anthemis tinctoria* 'E. C. Buxton', the distinct foliage in the foreground is *Helleborus x hybridus*.

BIOGRAPHY Katie Lukas (born 1950) is in the long and eminent line of gardeners, nursery proprietors, and others with plant knowledge, whose design skills are as much to do with advising their clients and helping them manage, "edit", bring back to life, or sometimes bring under control, their gardens and borders, as it is with designing from scratch. Indeed, Katie actually says she does not like starting with a blank canvas – which sets her apart from those who are first and foremost designers. Katie has been helping garden owners get to grips with their acres from one end of Britain to another since the early 1990s. I like to think of her as a modern-day Norah Lindsay – a genteel lady designer who, in the 1930s, went from country house to country house: advising, planning and planting, and whose own garden (at Sutton Courtney in Oxfordshire) became famous in its own right. Both share an avoidance of anything to do with "hard landscaping" (as do I).

"I never intended to run a business... I have no training, I have learnt everything by experience," says Katie, which is a classically British way of establishing a career. Although, she does confess to having done a five-day course in planning at the English Gardening School, she adds, "I'm rather dyslexic." Buying plants for clients involved getting to know a wide range of nurseries, and in 1996 she started what has turned out to be a very successful series of plant sales, bringing together often geographically far-flung nurseries and the plant-hungry British gardening public.

distant vistas, but also by creating a less intensely planted area of long meadow grass and young trees, from where it is possible to appreciate the surrounding landscape of marshy meadows and venerable-looking pollarded willows. This area is reached through a feature that dramatically illustrates Katie's consummate skill in using plant knowledge to serve design ends. It is a line of *Carpinus betulus* 'Fastigiata', a variety of hornbeam whose branches sweep elegantly upright; the top and sides are clipped straight, but the gaps between the trees naturally adopt the shape of a gothic arch. The result is an imposing, very architectural arched wall of foliage that sweeps across the garden in the way a viaduct does across a landscape.

"I garden for all seasons," says Katie, putting her finger on an aspect of garden design that many of the more architectural members of the profession often fail to consider. "In particular,

I have managed to get a bulb flowering for every month of the year." Tulips in spring make a particular splash, with their intense colours picking out similar but more subtly expressed shades in nearby flowers or leaves; in the autumn, she uses dahlias in the same way. Plants are combined and managed in order to get as much interest into a given space as possible; much is arranged in layers, so that space is used several times over – an example is the way she lifts the canopy of shrubs by pruning out lower branches, so that there is more space beneath them for underplanting with bulbs, like chionodexas, scillas, crocuses or smaller daffodils, or spring-flowering perennials such as pulmonarias or epimediums. It is tricks like this that only the experience of living with a garden can teach you, which makes Stone House such a valuable resource for the constant improvement of clients' gardens.

A ROBUST moisture-loving plant, *Primula florindae* has a deliciously spicy scent; when happy it can self-seed profusely. Plants of wet places can be somewhat rank and untidy in growth later in the season, which makes the presence of those relishing the conditions but having a better sense of structure so useful, such as the blue-grey leaved *Hosta sieboldiana* 'Elegans' here. In this garden, however, hedging and clipped order are never far away.

Some Favourite Plants

Acer pensylvanicum

A "snakebark" maple that Katie describes as being "beautiful at all times of year" for the delicate patterning of grey and red-brown stripes on the trunk of young trees and branches. The leaves turn yellow in autumn. Upright habit to 10m (33ft), and it appreciates shelter from wind, and moist, but well-drained soil. ZONE 4 MIN.

Clematis viticella 'Perle d'Azur'

An old variety, bred in France in 1885, and something of a classic, with light purple-blue flowers around 10cm (4in). It climbs up to a maximum of 3.5m/11ft (Katie grows it on hoops to just above head height), and is noted as looking particularly good with roses, flowering from early summer to early autumn. Likes sun or light shade, and the roots appreciate cool, moist, but well-drained, soil. ZONE 3 MIN.

Crocus speciosus

The purple flowers of this crocus "always appear much later than you think," observes Katie, "often not until October." The leaves do not appear until spring. Very useful for borders or thin grass, where an autumnal surprise is appreciated. Any well-drained soil in full sun or light shade. ZONE 6 MIN.

Elaeagnus angustifolia **'Quicksilver'** (Russian olive)

"The scent of the flowers is better than jasmine," says Katie of this deciduous silver-leaved shrub – it has been said that the young shoots look like they have been dipped in aluminium. The tiny yellow flowers are produced in mid-summer, while the foliage makes a good backdrop for a range of other plants through the growing season. Growing to 4m (13ft), preferring full sun and tolerant of all except very wet soils. Regarded as dangerously invasive in North America. ZONE 4 MIN.

Rosa 'Shropshire Lass'

A robust shrub rose, well-clothed in lush green foliage, with flat, almost single flowers in a delicate shade of pink that fade to white, followed by good hips – at Stone House it clambers over a potting shed roof – to 1.8m (6 ft) tall. Sun or very light shade, most soils, but particularly successful on clay. ZONE 4 MIN.

Stipa gigantea

One of the best ornamental grasses, forming a dense clump of narrow, dark evergreen leaves to around 50cm (20in). Tall and immensely airy heads of panicles shoot up to 2m (6½ft) – these look good from early summer to late autumn, and are best seen backlit against a dark background. Even once the seed heads are tatty by mid-winter, its tussocks of dark green "still have wonderful architecture," observes Katie. Long-lived and reliable in full sun and well-drained soils. ZONE 5 MIN.

Ulf Nordfjell Summerhouse, Umeå, Sweden

SITUATED IN A COUNTRYSIDE of forests and meadows, the garden at Ulf's summerhouse was cultivated together with his mother for some 30 years. "My mother was interested in producing food, growing vegetables, but she also had a brilliant eye for planting," says Ulf. The garden is typical of Swedish country gardens in its simplicity and understatement, seeming to merge with the trees of the surrounding landscape, and centred around a very characteristic house, painted in the traditional dark red paint that is used for the majority of country houses and nearly all agricultural buildings. There are few indications of the sophisticated design that is more typical of Ulf's commissioned work; this feels like a garden that is not only about his roots but also national roots.

"In Sweden," says Ulf, "we still have wild flower meadows close to cities, so we don't need to introduce theoretical floras such as prairies. We can go into the meadows and find geraniums, *Lilium martagon*, species of *Trifolium* (clover), campanulas, *Convallaria majalis* (lily of the valley) and *Caltha palustris* (kingcup) following the river. I always try to unite the wild and the more horticultural." Stepping outside this garden, you will find a profusion of wild plants within a few metres.

FERNS flourish in northern Sweden's cool climate; this is the spreading *Matteucia struthiopteris*. The red paint is very traditionally Swedish – made from milk, linseed oil and red ochre, it is an effective 'natural' defence against decay.

BIOGRAPHY Winning the 2009 "Best in Show" award at the Chelsea Flower Show gave international recognition to Ulf Nordfjell, a landscape architect who works almost entirely in his native Sweden. His homeland is, of course, renowned for its design, but not for its gardens – perhaps this will change; contrary to the opinion of many outsiders, its northern climate is not at all unfavourable to garden making. Ulf's private garden designs combine clean lines, for which Scandinavian design is famous, with highly effective plant combinations.

Dressed in black, Ulf fulfils the popular image of a designer. However, the nature of his career is very different to that of most garden designers. It is divided between working for Ramböll, an engineering company, where he works with other landscape architects and engineers on large-scale, architectural and landscape projects, and working for both private and public clients on garden and park design. "Actually, it's more like 100 per cent of my time on each half of my career," he says. One reason why Ulf divides his time like this is the freedom of making choices and working all the way from ideas to seeing them fulfilled. Another is typically Swedish: "I prefer to work for public projects, for bigger groups of people"; this is a country where the sense of the importance of the public good is highly developed, and where the cult of the individual ego is discouraged. "I like to work in networks," he says.

Ulf was brought up in Umeå, some 250km (155 miles) from the Arctic Circle. He spent holidays in the countryside outside Umeå. A childhood surrounded by nature led to an early interest in plants; as a teenager he became interested in design through studying and making ceramics. His first degree was in biology, the second in landscape architecture – a combination that has proved extremely useful when it comes to dealing with habitat-based plantings. A love of plants and hands-on gardening has stayed with him, but he says, "I am not a plant collector, I did that when I was in my early twenties, by twenty-five I became more interested in the social relations between plants."

One of the most important roles Ulf has made for himself has been that of garden festival organiser, most recently in the western city of Gothenburg in 2008. This, and a previous garden festival in the city in 2000, and the Garden and Arts and Crafts Festival 1998 in Stockholm, have done more than anything else to bring modern Swedish garden and planting design to the attention of the outside world, as well as to bring other leading European designers to Sweden.

GARDENS OPEN TO THE PUBLIC

All in Sweden

- **Umedalen Sculpture Gardens**, Spa park Umeå

- **Wij Gardens**, Ockelbo

- **Linnaeus Garden** (Chelsea Flower Show garden, 2007), Gothenburg Botanic Garden

- **Rose garden**, Tradsgårdsforenigen, Gothenburg

- **The Garden Society Garden** in Linköping

Ulf says that he spends about ten weeks here during the spring and summer, and only occasionally visits in winter, "but I do a lot of work here. I designed the 2009 Chelsea garden from here last summer, for instance… the place gives me the right to think. In my office in Stockholm there are so many things going on, meetings and the many public projects take up all the time."

A lawn creates a central restful space around which grow nepeta, varieties of *Hemerocallis* (day lily) and salvias (such as *S. nemorosa* 'Caradonna'), *Alchemilla mollis*, *cimicifugas*, ferns and delphiniums. On the terrace a few clipped boxes in containers and tubs of agapanthus suggest that the owner is more interested than average, for these do need winter protection. Large clumps of ostrich fern (*Matteucia struthiopteris*) appear to make a link with the wild surroundings – in fact, they are a legacy of Ulf's mother's planting, and are continuing to spread. A bank behind the house is densely planted with a profusion of herbaceous plants. In all, the gardened area is about 1,000 sq m (10,764 sq ft); in addition there are natural areas of around 1,500 sq m (16,146 sq ft). In some Swedish

TALL YELLOW *Hemerocallis lilioaspodelus* and purple *Nepeta x faassenii* (left) make an impact during early to mid-summer. They are amongst the perennials whose period of maximum growth coincides with the long days of the northern summer. Only perennials that do not mind cool nights will thrive at this latitude. The purple heliotrope alongside the hosta (above) can only be used as a summer annual.

gardens, it is difficult for outsiders to "read" the boundary between garden and surrounding nature – but here the boundary is actually very strict, and the absence of fences and other clear boundary markers gives an illusion of continuity.

Those unfamiliar with northern latitudes might be surprised at just how much can be grown here. But there is an advantage to growing this far north – the summer light. Plants are exposed to very long hours of daylight from May to July, a period of maximum growth for many species. Nights can be cold, however, which limits the growth of some perennials and summer plants, especially those from warm climates such as dahlias, or from severe continental climates where

growing seasons are short but very warm and humid. Many of the most familiar, late-flowering, herbaceous plants – for example, some species of Aster and *Solidago* (golden rods) – are from parts of North America; most will flourish and flower reasonably well at the latitude of Stockholm (59°north) but not this far north (63°).

"There is an incredible growth rate for those plants that can use the light," says Ulf. "Delphiniums grow to 2.2m (7ft), peonies and aconitums also grow well. There is a period of intense flowering, as the light brings on a wide variety of species to flower at once." A lack of summer heat limits the ripening of the wood of many tree species, so, Ulf says, "it is impossible to grow fruit trees." The visual quality of the light is, of course, delicate, even "fragile", so "purple and whites glitter."

"I test plants before I use them," Ulf explains. "If it survives here, then it will be fine further south." He adds that during the 1970s and 1980s, at a branch of the Swedish Agricultural University at Alnarp (near the southern tip of Sweden), there was a major study of plant provenance[1], which produced a list of recommended woody plants (the E-plant system); it is being continually updated. "Since then I have always been experimenting with these plants," says Ulf, but "so much depends on the weather… it can be -30°C (-22° F) for a week, if there is 50cm (20in) of snow it protects plants from cold, but if there is only 10cm (4in) then there is catastrophe."

This is a place to make the most of the brief, but intense, northern summer. It is a good reminder that it is not impossible to garden in the North.

1 "Provenance" refers to the geographic origin of the cultivated gene pool of a plant – this may vary greatly with altitude and latitude. There is, not surprisingly, a much greater tendency for plants whose ancestors came from high altitude or latitude to be more cold-tolerant.

Looking out from the garden, planted perennials seem to merge with the surrounding landscape.

Some Favourite Plants

Alchemilla mollis

One of the most common herbaceous plants of northern European gardens, the alchemilla is appreciated for the beautiful scallop shape of its leaves on which drops of water roll like beads of mercury, as well as for its green-yellow flower heads, the perfect foil to so many early summer flower colours. Growing to 50cm (20in) high and steadily spreading, it also has a tendency to self-seed. Any soil, sun or light shade. ZONE 4 MIN.

Astrantia 'Claret'

Astrantias are perennials that produce interestingly shaped flower heads around 2–3cm (¾–1¼in) across, surrounded by distinctive bracts. Generally greeny-creamy white, this cultivar is one of several dark red ones. It has a long, summer-flowering period and is a very good cut flower. Any soil, in sun or part shade, but dislikes drought. Happiest in cooler climates, where it generally self-seeds. ZONE 6 MIN.

Calamagrostis x *arundinacea* 'Karl Foerster'

One of the very best ornamental grasses, particularly for its long season of clear vertical emphasis, this variety flowers around mid-summer, with seed heads that continue to stand until well into winter. The height varies from 1.5 to 2m (5 to 6½ft), depending on soil fertility. Any soil, but full sunlight is absolutely essential. ZONE 4 MIN.

Euphorbia dulcis 'Chamaelon'

The dark bronze-red of the foliage of this small (40cm/15 ½in high) herbaceous euphorbia makes a great impact in spring, particularly alongside the blues and yellows of bulbs and other spring flowers. It self-sows in most gardens, but although healthy in northern Sweden, often suffers from mildew in warmer climates. Sun or light shade, any soil that is not too dry. ZONE 6 MIN.

Gillenia trifoliata

Subtlety is the keyword with the look of this woodland edge perennial. Fresh green leaves are joined by small white flowers on distinct red stems in early to mid-summer. It is delicate, almost ethereal, but a strong-growing and long-lived plant, reaching a height of around 1m (3ft). Light shade, moist, but well-drained soils. ZONE 4 MIN.

Salvia nemorosa 'Caradonna'

A relatively new variety from a thoroughly reliable and tough group of perennials, this is of a more compact habit (to 50cm/20in high) than many other sages, with violet-blue flowers on purple stems. It flowers in early spring, and again later in the summer, if it is deadheaded. Likes any well-drained soils, including dry ones, sun. This is not a "perennial" perennial, often dying after 3–5 years. ZONE 4 MIN.

Christine Orel, The Garden in Herzogenaurach, Bavaria, Germany

CHRISTINE HERSELF is now "between gardens", living in a flat overlooking Herzogenaurach's medieval high street, and balancing being a single parent, running a design practice and her commitment to the choir – a garden at the moment is just too much to take on. Until recently she lived on the edge of town, with a medium-sized garden (750 sq m/8,073 sq ft) surrounding a house that was built in the 1990s, but in a traditional Franconian (north Bavarian) style. The garden, divided into two, reflected the dual purpose of the house, as family home and office. The lower part was used as the "the office garden" where Christine and her staff could sit outside in a sheltered sun trap in the morning or at lunchtime, and the upper part, which is west-facing and gets the evening sun, was for family use.

The garden is too small for serious trialling of plants, and has very much been a personal garden, reflecting the stress Christine puts on combining carefully designed hard elements and an interesting mix of plant varieties, together with her clear appreciation of good garden practice. Only a dedicated gardener would put in the time necessary to develop a wisteria "tree", where what is usually a climber is turned into a standard, through skilled and frequent pruning, and the support of a metal framework. The garden also

CHRISTINE may be queen of the colour combination, but her gardens often feature walls and steps built of massive stones – particularly where there is a need for a retaining wall. In her own garden she has entirely used stone from an architectural salvage depot.

BIOGRAPHY "*Aruncus dioicius* 'Horatio' planted with *Penstemon digitalis* 'Husker's Red' makes me think of the opening of Wagner's *Parsifal*" – you only have to spend a few minutes with Christine Orel (born 1962) to realise that she really wanted to be a musician. She has been passionate about music since childhood, as an instrumentalist (piano) and singer, particularly as a member of various choirs. Her career in garden and landscape design developed because of a regular holiday job that she had in a nursery as a teenager. Music provides many of the metaphors she uses to think and talk about planting design – harmonies, disharmonies, melodies and rhythms. She even relates particular colours to particular notes – yellow she thinks of as E major, blue as A major. "It is possible," she says, "to plant something that has the character of music. I have done a pop garden, a jazz garden and a rock (music) garden."

Christine describes her work portfolio as being 40 per cent private garden, 40 per cent garden show and 20 per cent corporate. Until 2008, she worked on her own, with two to four employees, but she has now teamed up with another designer, Andreas Heidrich. Garden shows are a particular feature of German gardening life; at least three or four are held every summer in different places; summer-long events that are designed not just to be three month wonders, but to leave a permanent legacy in the form of an infrastructure and planting for a public park. Christine's design office in Herzogenaurach near Nürnberg is involved in creating plantings for many of these shows, sometimes on their own, sometimes in collaboration with other designers, Plantings in Germany are very definitely either annual or perennial – the characteristic perennial style is now relatively familiar outside the country, the annual less so. The annual plantings are amazingly eclectic, using every category of plant: true annuals, tender perennials, vegetables, grasses, wild flowers and bulbs, to create complex symphonies of colour, shape and texture.

Christine's forte is to create harmonious blends of plants. As she points out, "everyone always sees colour first; colour and form cannot exist without each other. I want to write a text 'thinking in black and white'… without vertical and horizontal repetition, colour is uninteresting." There are always strong structures in Christine's gardens – repeated box balls or low hedging, although their organisation is usually modernist in feel. "I hope I'm not influenced by anybody," she says, but then checks herself. "Oh dear, that sounds arrogant… but I designed several borders before I saw any pictures of English gardens. I then discovered Gertrude Jekyll… I think that if people think about plants and colour a lot, they will end up doing similar things."

illustrates her skill in using stones for hard surfaces — all the granite paving slabs and smaller setts for paths and seating areas have been sourced from salvage dealers.

Yew hedging surrounds much of the garden and divides it into rooms. At the rear, a gate is cleverly hidden by an extension to the outer yew hedge, a simple design trick, but only rarely seen. Further structure is provided by occasional box balls, which indeed make a frequent appearance in Christine's gardens. With a slope of 4.5m (14 ¾ft) from top to bottom, steps are occasionally necessary — these are granite, to match the paving. One set of steps leads down to a small vegetable garden that occupies a warm-looking south-facing terrace.

Christine is renowned for her adventurous use of colour in plantings. However, in this garden she has mostly worked with more traditional colour mixes — pink roses with purple-mauve varieties of nepeta, allium, geranium and lavender, white campanulas and achillea. Tulips in spring are an opportunity to add more daring flashes of colour. But beneath all there are good bones — this is a garden that would photograph well in black and white.

COLOUR combinations have to take their cue from key components. Roses work well as the starting point of pastel colour mixes, but companion plants need to be tolerant of some root competition and summer drought.

Some Favourite Plants

Acanthus mollis

Seen by some as coarse and invasive, Christine appreciates the majestic size and cut of the leaves of a perennial that was immortalised by the stone carvers of ancient Greek temples. Muscular-looking flower heads of purple and white appear in early to mid-summer, followed by robust seed heads. Foliage grows to 80cm (31in) high, flowers to 1.5m (5ft), and it strongly spreads, if happy. Likes fertile soil in full sun or light shade. Summer-dormant in dry conditions. ZONE 6 MIN.

Heuchera villosa var. macrorrhiza

Heucheras have become popular perennials in recent years for the coloured foliage of a range of hybrids – this naturally occurring variety, however, has lush green leaves, and makes its presence felt more through the form of its hunky shape. Christine values its "fresh green very early in the year, and spikes of white flowers in August, they remind me of candles" – to 80cm (31in) in height. Light shade, or full sun, if drought is not a problem. ZONE 6 MIN.

Panicum virgatum 'Heavy Metal'

This is one of several varieties of the prairie grass that has proven the most successful in European gardens. Blue-toned foliage, and an upright habit, make this variety particularly useful in borders. It has heads of immensely fine flowers (and later seeds) in autumn, persisting well through the winter – to 1.5m (5ft) tall. Enjoys fertile soil and full sun, some drought tolerance. ZONE 4 MIN.

Penstemon digitalis 'Husker's Red'

Whilst most penstemons are grown for their flowers, this one is more valued for its broad leaves, which are dark green, flushed bronze-red. In contrast, the flowers are white, with a tinge of pink – to 60cm (23½in) tall. Unlike most penstemons, this is truly herbaceous, so there is no need for pruning. Likes full sun, and is relatively drought-tolerant. ZONE 3 MIN.

Persicaria bistorta 'Superba'

A large form of a common European wild flower, this strong-growing plant of moist soils produces a flurry of pale pink flower spikes in early summer, and very often, another set in late summer, especially if mown in mid-summer – to 80cm (31in) in height, spreading vigorously. Likes sun or light shade, fertile and moist, even wet, soils. ZONE 3 MIN.

Astilbe chinensis var. taquetii 'Superba'

Astilbes are favourite plants for damp soil, in either sun or light shade. Most are rather stiff in bearing; this one, however, is more relaxed in habit, and, at up to 1.2m (4ft) high, rather majestic; it is also more tolerant of drier soils. Attractive, much-divided leaves and soft purple-pink fluffy flowers in early summer, and rather impressive seedheads for autumn and winter. ZONE 4 MIN.

Piet Oudolf Hummelo, Netherlands

I FIRST VISITED Piet and Anja Oudolf and their garden at Hummelo in the eastern Netherlands in the summer of 1994. I've been back annually most years I think, so I've seen it change and develop, and in many different weathers: chilled by winter winds hurtling out of Siberia, flooded, warmed by spring sunlight, baked by a harsher, summer sun. One thing it always keeps is its sense of structure – the distinctive yew curtains at the end of the garden, a number of yew hedges and a beech tunnel about half way down the 4,050 sq m (1 acre) front garden have been permanent fixtures.

Piet's career started out in the very architectural tradition of garden modernism, and the garden in its earlier years reflected that. "In the early years there was Mien Ruys and that was it," he explains. Ruys (1904–99) was the Bauhaus-modernist style garden architect who dominated post-war Dutch design, but whose background as the daughter of a nurseryman also ensured that she used plants creatively. A central axis plunged down between staggered yew columns through the middle of three oval borders, whose axes were oddly off-centre. Roy Strong, visiting in the late 1990s, summed it all up almost as soon as he stepped off his tour bus – "wonky baroque".

UNTIL 2003, the rear part of the Oudolf garden looked like this – the off-centre symmetry and blocks of planting (the silver is *Stachys byzantina*) reflecting the architectural focus which underlay Piet's work. Now the grass and central border have been dug up and replaced by a more naturalistic perennial planting. The yew 'curtains' at the rear remain, however – they have almost become the trademark of this garden.

BIOGRAPHY Piet Oudolf (born 1944) trained as a garden designer at the age of 25, and went on to develop a reputation as an imaginative creator of gardens, mostly urban and suburban. His main influence was Mien Ruys, a garden designer whose Bauhaus-influenced architectural style dominated Dutch design for much of the latter half of the 20th century.

Growing steadily more interested in plants, Piet began to make visits to English and German gardens and nurseries, eventually deciding that he needed his own nursery to grow the plants his design schemes required. Moving to Hummelo (in the eastern province of Gelderland) in 1981, he began to accumulate a collection of plants that, after trialling and some selection work, was narrowed down to form the basis of the distinctive palette of plants he uses today. Meanwhile, his wife Anja began to develop the retail side of the nursery, which soon began to acquire a formidable reputation amongst amateur gardeners for exciting new plants. Whilst the Dutch knew him as the designer who also sold plants, British gardeners first knew him as a nurseryman who also designed gardens.

Piet's style began to move away from the architectural Mien Ruys look, as herbaceous plants took centre stage, especially late summer perennials and grasses. He began to popularise what he believed to be the decorative look of seed heads and dead foliage in winter, and with some skilful photography of his garden covered in hoar frost, he simultaneously started a trend in both garden photography and planting design.

The last ten years have seen a steady increase in the number of projects undertaken outside The Netherlands, particularly in public spaces in the USA, and for large gardens open to the public in Britain. However, his first park planting was at Enkjöping in Sweden in 1996.

Piet's work always included imaginative elements of what perhaps might be best described as "neo-formalism" – the Dutch tradition of shaping and clipping plants is a strong one. That said, recent years have seen less of this, and more focus on advancing herbaceous planting design – which is now reflected in the Hummelo garden, where the central axis is now all but invisible beneath planting. Piet explains, "We once had a series of yew columns down the axis of the garden, but as they grew I realised I had too many, so began to take them out, although some I turned into 'yew tables' – a surreal element." Flooding eventually killed them and they were all removed. The water table is usually about 1 metre/yard below the surface, but the garden is at the lowest point of the neighbourhood and so it is vulnerable to winter flooding. The loss of such permanent structural elements has meant a growing emphasis on herbaceous plants and grasses for structure, rather than woody plants – even the central axial path has now gone, and has been replaced by three circles of herbaceous planting. Piet's growing appreciation of the visual value of herbaceous plants in winter goes hand in hand with good horticultural practice – one winter's flooding can destroy years, or decades, of woody plant growth, whereas perennials and grasses can recover quickly, or be replaced.

The Hummelo garden is the one garden that is not planned on the big sheets of tracing paper he uses for clients' gardens. "I do not draw plans for our own garden," he says, "but I make lists, and work out a concept in my mind, and then set plants out by eye." For the most part he eschews traditional "front and back" borders, so plants have to look good from a variety of angles. Brick paths dictate that visitors tend to walk around in circles, which means that viewpoints are always

changing; in particular there is a strong sense that plants are being looked over, rather than at, and in many cases the geography of paths and planting ensures that the viewer is much closer to plants than in more conventional gardens.

The garden is partly a showpiece – potential clients are invited here, and the garden can be seen by the many visitors to the nursery, which Anja runs behind the house. Its frequent appearance in magazine articles also means that it is a garden which really is something of a shop window. It is also a trial plot, as Piet explains: "I work in so many different spaces, have so many new ideas, I try out many ideas elsewhere, and so often want to change the garden at home as well. It is also very important to show people my ideas."

Many new plants are tried out here. Plant selection is perhaps the core of Piet's work; it

provides the vocabulary for a language of planting design, which continues to develop and grow. Fortunately, his plant palette, and other similar species are increasingly available, making it possible for others to experiment with the new wave of perennial planting too.

September is probably the best time to see Piet and Anja's garden. It is when the largest number of plants is at their best – and biggest. The sheer size and lushness of many of the plants is one thing that always amazes me. But there is an extraordinary amount of delicacy and subtlety too: ultra-fine grass flower heads, and threadlike stems with clouds of minute flowers. There are pale and understated colours amongst much brighter ones, backed by an incredible range of textures, of leaves, stems and seed heads. For anyone who loves plants, it is a magical

THIS LATE summer border is one of the longest lasting features of Piet's original garden. With the dimensions and basic form of a classic herbaceous border, it plays with a very different plant mix, including many grasses. The pink at the rear is *Eupatorium maculatum* 'Atropurpureum'.

experience; the opportunity to walk along narrow paths and feel immersed in plantings that combine so much beauty, with so much diversity, to appreciate the familiar, well-grown and displayed, alongside the joy of meeting the unfamiliar.

Structure is provided by grasses and perennials, which have been selected for a long period of architectural interest. A lot of colour,

however, is provided by what Piet calls "filler" species, which are rather amorphous but fill space and flower plentifully – geraniums are the most obvious example. A rough rule for planting design, Piet suggests, is about 70 per cent "structural" (plants with a long season of good form) and 30 per cent filler. Ensuring such a mix means that even in the depths of winter there is plenty to admire.

AUTUMN SEES a gradual falling apart of summer's order; seedheads and grasses play an important role now – the popularisation of these as late garden features has been one of the major influences of Piet's career. Dew on spider webs reminds us how important the late season border is to wildlife.

TIMELINE

1981 Piet and family moved in, developing the area around the house (then the fields, and some unkempt shrubs) for stock plant and trial beds.

1987 The distinctive yew "curtains" at the rear of the front garden were created. Originally comprising a nursery bed of young yew plants, most of them were removed, leaving the remainder to be shaped into what has become a trademark feature of the garden.

1993 Main layout was completed, including the beech tunnel – half of which was already there.

1996 Extensive flooding was followed by a re-development of the central axis of the garden with three off-centre beds, and a series of borders at the sides.

2003 All the lawn in the rear part of the garden was taken out and replaced by perennials, with a series of brick paths to allow access.

THE PALE pink flowers of Pink *Astrantia major* 'Roma' is the centrepiece of this planting. The garden at Hummelo has always been a blend of the favourite and the unfamiliar, or those such as astrantias, which were once grown only by specialists but now have mass appeal – thanks to designers like Piet. Piet continues to be actively involved with the selection of new perennial varieties for commercial development.

Some Favourite Plants

Amsonia species

Amsonias have steely-blue flowers in early summer, atop upright stems clothed in narrow leaves – very narrow in the case of *A.hubrechtii*. Forming steadily expanding clumps with stems around 1m (3ft) tall, amsonias have a late-season bonus – good yellow autumn colour. They combine particularly well with geraniums and enjoy full sun, with fertile soils. MOST SPECIES ZONE 5 MIN.

Selinum tenuifolium

An umbellifer, grown more for the elegant, lacelike structure of its flowers and seed heads, atop 1m (3ft) high stems, than for its colour (cream). The foliage, too, has a lacy quality. Combine with aconitum, filipendula and phlox. Short-lived but usually self-sows in sun or light shade. ZONE 6 MIN.

Deschampsia cespitosa

One of the earliest grasses to perform, this clump-forming, native north European species and its cultivars form clouds of tiny flowers in early summer, which develop into fawn seed heads for the autumn and early winter. In addition, the dense clumps of dark leaves are a valuable winter feature. Good repetition plant for borders – to 80cm (2½ft) high and across. ZONE 4 MIN.

Salvia nemorosa, S. x *superba* cultivars and hybrids

Mostly available in blues, purples and violets, the European salvias are not only colourful but also have good structure (at least while they flower). Most will perform again in autumn if dead headed – to 40–60cm (1½–2ft) high. They combine well with *achillea*, *origanum* and *stipa* grasses. Mid-blue 'Dear Anja', which Piet raised himself, is a particular favourite, but at nearly 1m (3ft) it is taller than most. Enjoys sun, any soil and is drought tolerant. ZONE 6 MIN.

Stachys officinalis

A north-European wildflower, with neat clumps of spreading foliage and small spikes of flower, *Stachys officinalis* reaches a height of 40cm (1½ft). 'Rosea' is an attractive pale pink, 'Hummelo' is a taller and more upright variety with dark lilac flowers. The original species is as good as any of these with deep violet flowers. Sun or light shade, preferring slightly moister soils. ZONE 5 MIN.

Veronicastrum species and cultivars

A tall (1.6m/5¼ft) genus for early summer, with tiny flowers densely packed on upwardly thrusting spikes – mauve, pink or white, depending on cultivar. After the flowers have faded, it is still an arresting plant for its vertical lines. Good with *echinacea* and phlox. Enjoys full sun and fertile soil. ZONE 3 MIN.

Mien Ruys Moerheimstraat, Netherlands

O F ALL THE gardens in this book, this is the only one where a designer has spent all of her life. She became actively involved in shaping her parents' garden at the age of nineteen, when she removed an old orchard and set out a new path. It is also a garden that has been extensively and systematically used for design experiments – for around 70 years.

The garden is some 2.4 hectares (6 acres), divided into 28 plots. Design laboratory it may have been, but it does not feel like it; there is a sense of space, with enough areas of lawn and woodland to create restful breaks between the more intensely planted or hard landscaped areas.

Representing most of the different styles that Ruys played with over the years, it is a good place, for both aspiring designers and amateur gardeners, to visit to get ideas – particularly for British and North American gardeners, who have seen little of the impact of modernism at home. The wide use of plants, and the importance that Ruys clearly placed in experimenting with new plants, or using familiar ones in novel ways fascinates plant-loving gardeners, all too often alienated by a seeming lack of interest in plants shown by many designers.

An area called the "Old Experimental Border" started off as a double border based on the colour

REPEATING SQUARES – as a pond, blocks of box or of grasses, within a context defined by regular paving and formally-trimmed hedges; this is the modernist version of the formal tradition in western garden design.

BIOGRAPHY Dutch landscape architect Mien Ruys (1904–99) was one of the most prolific and one of the most influential garden designers of the 20th century – yet there is very little published about her in English. Her father was proprietor of the Royal Moerheim Nurseries, one of the largest herbaceous plant nurseries in The Netherlands. After studying in Germany and England, she began designing gardens in the 1920s, leaving a portfolio of around 3,000 designs by the time she died in 1999.

From 1928 onwards, Ruys's style was heavily influenced by the modernist architecture group, the *Congrès International d'Architecture Moderne* (CIAM) – the membership included Le Corbusier. In the words of compatriot Piet Oudolf, her modernist style "completely dominated all post-war garden design." Until 1945, most of her work was for large private gardens, which included the extensive use of herbaceous plants, but in the post-war era she undertook many public or communal projects, with a greater emphasis on space and hard landscaping. During this period, her signature style was the use of paths and visual axes that were oblique to the dominant axis of the shape of the space or the surrounding architecture.

Like all modernists, Mien Ruys aimed for simplicity and clean lines, but unlike most of her colleagues she always liked to use a wide variety of plants, preferably in loose, informal combinations. By the 1960s, however, her work showed a change towards more perpendicular lines and a greater willingness to confine or clip plants into geometric formations. Ruys loved experimenting with

new materials, popularising the use of concrete tiles in the 1950s and railway sleepers in the 1960s – the latter went on to become one of the most popular "modern" garden ingredients of the late 20th century. She was also a prolific writer – helped by a publisher husband, with whom she started the magazine *Onze Eigen Tuin* (our own garden), which is still running.

Ruys may have made private gardens for the rich and famous, but she always had strong sympathies for modernist and socialist ideas. Her reputation was as an ascetic and workaholic – living in Spartan conditions and reputedly saying, "There are only two things I can make, gardens and tea".

GARDENS OPEN TO
THE PUBLIC

• **Tuinen Mien Ruys,**
Dedemsvaart,
Netherlands

theories of Jekyll, which Ruys then made changes to over the years, tweaking the colour combinations. This is the most self-consciously flowery and traditional part of the garden. Elsewhere, grasses are frequent, as Ruys was one of the first designers to start using them – her father was a good friend of the German nurseryman and writer Karl Foerster (1874–1970), who initially popularised their use. Perennials with bold or distinctive foliage make frequent appearances, such as bergenias, aralias and the majestic Japanese vine, *Vitis coignetiae*.

In Ruys's younger days, herbaceous plants were used almost entirely in borders, with an emphasis on the flowers. Foerster began the process of encouraging gardeners to look to other aspects of their personalities – form, foliage and texture – but Ruys completed the process. Low-

growing species, whose main visual impact is their foliage, are now a key part of planting design, especially for corporate or other public projects. Many such plants were first used here: species of *Bergenia*, *Alchemilla*, *Phlomis russeliana* and the grass *Hakonechloa macra*. A large block of *Phlomis russeliana* is part of one of the most visually striking areas in the garden. This is the Yellow Garden, where a perfect circle of grass surrounded by a brick path is bordered for most of the way by yellow-flowered plants.

One of the most striking aspects of both Piet Oudolf's and Mien Ruys's work is the use of geometrically clipped shrubs in a modernist rather than a traditional way. In some places hedges, or architectural blocks of box, yew or various species of *Berberis* dominate, creating an atmosphere of austere minimalism; in others, they appear

BUILT IN 1990, this naturalistic marsh garden contains mostly native species, such as yellow *Iris pseudacorus*. Access is on decking steps – made of recycled plastic. Mien Ruys was a pioneer in using new materials throughout her life.

THE Yellow Garden (1982) consists of a border of perennials in shades of yellow around a simply defined brick circle. The seedheads on the right are of *Phlomis russeliana*, which has deep golden flowers in early summer.

occasionally, as a structural element contrasting with loose herbaceous plantings. Grasses, too, sometimes appear in geometrically planted blocks.

Being located in The Netherlands means there has to be a water garden. Here, there is a mass of flag iris, reed mace, *Darmera peltata* and other native species, and the garden is accessible via a stepping-stone type boardwalk of recycled plastic. Other water bodies are smaller and much more formal – the kind of rather austere pool that has since been constructed in many thousands of gardens. Not all of Ruys's ideas have been taken up – for example, her minimal modern version of the pergola, designed to support climbers to act as a decorative screen, is not often seen.

The use of hard materials is one of the most distinctive aspects of modernist garden design, particularly in urban gardens. Ruys was a pioneer in this respect, and given the almost total lack of building stone in The Netherlands, she often looked to concrete as an alternative. Concrete has the advantage that it can be cast into an enormous variety of shapes, but the disadvantage that it has become so associated with an unpopular 1960s "brutalist" architectural and landscapes style that it is immediately read as dated and ugly. However, there is always a good case for going back to the source, to see how a material was used when it was fresh and new, as opposed to clichéd and abused. Concrete here is always used with subtlety, such as pavoirs alternating with grass, or as narrow strips bleeding into a lawn. There are concrete planters and even concrete furniture.

The Mien Ruys garden, which encapsulates so much of recent design history, and is so full of good ideas that we can still learn from it, has deservedly been given national monument status by the Dutch government. It is well worth the pilgrimage.

Some Favourite Plants

Anthriscus sylvestris with *Narcissus* 'Thalia'

Plant for early white bloom and the charm of wild flowers. Known as cow parsley, *Anthriscus* is a common European wild flower, typically seen in hedgerows in early summer. Despite weedy appearances it is a good garden plant, never overwhelming other species. Growing to around 1m (3ft), it thrives in light shade and fertile soil. The narcissus grows to around 40cm (16in) and is mid to late season. ZONE 3 MIN. *Anthriscus* is hardy to ZONE 5 MIN.

Euonymus alatus

A spreading shrub (2 x 3m/6½–10ft) with spectacular pink-red autumn colour and curious stems with corky winged appendages. Beatrice Krehl, who was head gardener here for many years, notes that a clipped, low hedge of this plant makes an effective block structure in the winter. Any soil in sun or light shade, out of cold winds; thrives on alkaline soils. ZONE 4 MIN.

Hosta sieboldiana 'Elegans'

One of the most elegant of hostas, the pleated and puckered leaves of 'Elegans' adds dignity to wherever it is planted. Reaches 1m (3ft) or more. Likes moist soils, part shade. As with all hostas, protection from slug and snail damage is vital. Sufficiently architectural to be popular in urns and other large containers, which is also a good way of defending them against molluscs. ZONE 4 MIN.

Lysimachia punctata

Many regard this old cottage garden plant as an aggressive weed, but Beatrice notes that "it is such a versatile plant Mien Ruys could use it in the sun and half shade, and you can manipulate the flowering season by cutting some stems back by a third". To 1m (3ft) tall and vigorously spreading in any fertile soil in sun or light shade. ZONE 4 MIN.

Metasequoia glyptostroboides

Beatrice tells us that this is "the living fossil tree – Moerheim got seed from the second collection in China." Today it is often planted as a street tree for its light deciduous foliage (despite being a conifer) and elegant narrow habit. To 20m (65ft) high by 6m (19½ft) across, any soil, especially moist or wet ones. It can also be clipped as a formal hedge, although this is rarely seen. ZONE 5 MIN.

Miscanthus x giganteus

The value of this big ornamental grass is that at Moerheim it blends in with wild reeds along the edge of water. It also makes a dramatic garden statement: 2.5m (8ft) high and slowly spreading, any soil in sun, including moist ones (but not waterlogged). A good companion for really big late-season perennials like Eupatorium maculatum and species of Helianthus. ZONE 4 MIN.

Lauren Springer Ogden & Scott Ogden

Fort Collins, Colorado & Austin, Texas, USA

LAUREN AND SCOTT have been together since 2002 and have kept both the houses and gardens they had when they met. However, whereas Scott's garden in Austin, Texas, was three years old, Lauren had only just started hers in Fort Collins, Colorado. The result, according to Lauren, is that "the Colorado garden has been more of a place we began together." "Lauren had to put up with more of my sacred cows at first," replies Scott, to which Lauren answers, "I've gotten rid of some of his sacred cows."

The Texas garden is, according to Scott, "almost sub-tropical, but varies between Saudi Arabia and Burma… winters are zone 8/9… the garden only 1,000 sq m (¼ acre) over chalk and three-quarters shaded by live oaks." The Colorado garden, also alkaline, is around twice the size, at 1,500 sq m (2/5 acre), in zone 5b; rainfall is low (annually around 400mm/16in) and summer nights generally cool. The Texan garden looks tropical, at least to the outsider, with palms, aloes, agaves and yuccas. The Colorado look, however, is unfamiliar to gardeners from temperate climates – bunch grasses dominate, and there are many compact grey, blue and silver shrubs, with the twiggy habit and diminutive foliage typical of drought-tolerant species, and prominent boulders, gravel and flagstone. The Colorado garden has an

SEVERAL SPECIES of wild tulip in flower. Many are from central Asia – an area with a very similar climate to Colorado. To successfully re-flower every year, species tulips need a thorough 'baking' from the sun and high nutrient levels. The dark red flower on the right is *Pulsatilla vulgaris* 'Rubra'.

BIOGRAPHY "Unfortunately, much of what is promoted as or called a garden in North America is nothing more than a landscape installation," write Lauren Springer Ogden and Scott Ogden, a husband-and-wife garden design team. Key to the couple's design work is their passion for plants, and how they see them as being central to gardens. Lauren (born 1959) worked as a professional gardener and propagator before turning to garden design. Scott (born 1957) has had a career as nurseryman, garden designer and consultant. They have a love of wild spaces, and their animals and plants are fundamental to both of them; as a consequence their garden-making is informed by a deep knowledge of wild habitats. Lauren's parents were both from central Europe, and as a child she spent summers hiking in the Alps, and developed a particular feel for mountain vegetation.

Both Lauren and Scott were widely respected garden writers before they met; since when they have started writing together. "Before we met, it was eerie how our books were in parallel," says Lauren. "We were each working in the interior of the country but with very different climates... we were both working in a vacuum, there was so little information or plants available." A 2008 collaboration says it all – *Plant-Driven Design*. Lauren and Scott clearly counterpoise their work against those who regard landscape design as primarily being about hard features: walls, paths and water features. They even take aim at two of the most hallowed names in 20th-century design, Thomas Church and Sylvia Crowe, for their lack of real interest in plants. Their practice is a small one; clients are mostly residential, although the couple have created a number of public gardens.

History will probably remember Lauren and Scott as the pioneers in designing with plants in climate zones that until now have received little attention: the great swathe of North America that reaches up from Texas to Saskatchewan, where low rainfall and often harsh winters combine to make for a particularly testing combination for conventional planting. This is the land of short-grass prairie, sagebrush steppe and other wild habitats, where tough, low-growing, drought-tolerant plants dominate. It is not just that Lauren and Scott make gardens that relate and belong to these landscapes, but that the harsh lessons of these climates have clearly led to a particularly disciplined approach to the relationship between plant and place.

GARDENS OPEN TO THE PUBLIC

- **Tropical Mosaic Garden** at Naples Botanical Garden in Florida

- **Water-Smart Garden, Romantic Gardens and others** at Denver Botanic Gardens (Colorado)

- **Sibley Conservatory renovation** at Callaway Gardens Resort, Pine Mountain, Georgia.

open and serene, yet full look, thanks to over 3,000 different plant species. The overlap in plants between the two gardens is only around 5 per cent, due to the cold in Colorado and the heat in Texas, although as Lauren notes, "we try to shift things around, a nightmare on the plane with plants in bags." Scott points out something interesting as regards the Texan species: "Historically the state has occasionally experienced very cold weather sweeping down from the Arctic, so many Texan natives have a genetic predisposition to hardiness. Many are successful in Colorado; in fact, make better garden plants, as spring is not so hot or over so quickly."

Scott continues, "In our own gardens we grow plants we get to enjoy, I get a kick out of watching plants grow, and we experiment and trial" – "we

kill a lot of plants," Lauren notes. The couple do all their own gardening and building with no outside help. "Back in the 1980s," recalls Scott, "the palette from nurseries for designing was paltry, so early on I started acquiring plants, digging up or propagating from abandoned gardens, collecting seed in the wild in Texas and in Mexico." Lauren recalls, "When I moved here twenty years ago, I was passionate about Colorado and regional natives, spending every weekend botanising and seed collecting. Since then there has been a real horticultural explosion in gardening, people on the coasts are now trying to grow our natives." The couple have introduced about a dozen cultivars into commerce and have made a real impact through selecting regional natives or other species suitable for their climates.

A FIREPIT in the centre of the garden provides a social space. In late summer, many grasses are looking at their best and the locally native biennial daisy-relative *Erigeron divergens* is in full flower.

Despite their love of natives, Lauren and Scott are by no means dogmatic nativists, muttering "bio-fascism" about those who preach that only plants from the immediate region should be used in planted landscapes. About half the plants in the Colorado garden are native to the North American interior, the rest are from regions with a similar climate: central Asia, the Mediterranean, the South African Drakensberg and Karoo.

"The garden is a typical suburban lot, but with nice views out to the foothills," explains Lauren. Scott is blunt about the passive solar house: "It's an uninspiring box. We've tried to make it sink into the background... one thing we did to help this was to plant an arbour, with lots of climbers: grapes, wisteria, honeysuckle."

Like most American gardens, lawn predominated when Lauren arrived – in a region where the survival of green grass is completely dependent upon irrigation. "My first action,"

explains Lauren, "was to spray off the lawn, then we planted trees, but not all of them have survived, but even so we have had to do some thinning out... the second year was planting up pretty much the whole area. From the first we had a strong idea of the spaces we wanted, and developed the plantings around them."

"I like my privacy, that's very important to me," says Lauren, "so in the smaller front, we've grown a screen, it's easier to water there and keep it lush." The rear garden, with its view to the mountains, is wilder and less irrigated. There are three zones here: reasonably moist (by Colorado standards), moderately dry and steppe. In the first there are grasses, such as *Deschampsia cespitosa*, *Sesleria heufleriana* and *S. autumnalis*, *Sporobolus heterolepis* (prairie drop seed), species of Carex, and small daffodils. The drier area, planted with apple and other fruit trees, uses more native grasses, such as *Schizachrium scoparium*, *Festuca*

THIS GRASS, so beautifully backlit, is *Deschampsia caespitosa*. "The fluffy spike seedheads," says Lauren, "are *Liatris punctata*, our locally native Prairie Gayfeather." In a dry climate like that of Colorado, seedheads can be a particularly effective winter feature.

idahoensis and *Koeleria macrantha*. There are a lot of bulbs here, particularly alliums and species of tulips – originally from central Asia, with a similar climate to Colorado. The steppe area is drier still, with dwarf species of *Festuca*, mixed in with species of *Artemisia*, bulbous iris, crocus and *Pulsatilla*.

There is no doubt that bunch grasses dominate much of the Colorado garden, a reflection of the way in which very similar species define much of the regional natural landscape. "I've been crazy about grasses since I was a kid," says Lauren, "but not everyone likes them, it is initially love or hate." Scott explains that "people are attracted to a meadow landscape, but think that they can just have it, not realising the amount of work involved." Many species are relatively slow to establish, and competition from alien weed or grass species can be a problem in the early phases.

It's always interesting to hear about how gardening couples get along, who does what and decides what. "I do most of the garden work," says Lauren cheerfully. "I am the work horse, the waterer, the weeder, the editor, the grunt, Scott more the researcher… we are both pretty alpha, but it has worked out fine." "We do the basic layout together," says Scott, and Lauren adds, "we usually agree." She went on to explain a basic ground rule about how they use the garden: "we photograph it for lectures and books, but we don't show it to clients… our garden is private, it's our haven."

A VARIETY of species of *Festuca* – an important genus of bunch grasses, especially successful in stressful habitats. The 'firework' at the rear is *F. mairei*. Festucas play an important role in this garden by evoking the texture of short-grass prairie, a major local plant community.

AUTUMN – with some of the colour for which the North American woody flora is famous. On the left is *Aesculus glabra* (Ohio buckeye), in the centre Serviceberry *Amelanchier canadensis*. The pale yellow tree is *Chionanthus virginicus* (Fringe tree). The blue conifer on the right is *Abies lasiocarpa* var. *arizonica*. The aster in the middle is *Symphyotrichum oblongifolium* (Aromatic Aster). Tree planting in Lauren's garden has been partly developed as a privacy screen from neighbouring properties.

Some Favourite Plants

Ericameria nauseosa var. *albicaulis* 'Santa Fe Silver'

With the wonderful name of rubber rabbit brush, this is a superior selection of a common shrub of dry soils in the American west. Growing to around 2m (6½ft) tall, it has narrow silver leaves on upwardly-swept white twiggy branches, and bright yellow flowers in loose clusters in autumn. Very drought tolerant. ZONE 5 MIN, HARDY TO -28°C (-20°F).

Yucca constricta

This elegant yucca has tightly packed narrow grey-green, filiferous foliage growing from a short-trunked rosette. White flowers on tall stems are produced on older plants. Full sun and very good drainage, it will survive dry cold to well below freezing, but not necessarily damp cold. ZONE 5 MIN, HARDY TO -26°C (-15°F).

Iris x histrioides 'Katharine Hodgkin'

An exquisitely beautiful early spring-flowering bulbous iris, with intense dark patterning on a pale blue background of a teal shade that is very rare in flowers; 20cm (8in) stems. Very well-drained soils in full sun are vital for success, as are dry conditions in summer. ZONE 5 MIN, HARDY TO -28°C (-20°F).

Origanum bracted hybrids

Closely related to the oregano, or marjoram of Mediterranean cooking, these are a steadily expanding group of hybrids useful for their flowering somewhat later in summer than many drought-tolerant perennials. Insignificant flowers are surrounded by showy pink or chartreuse hop-like bracts. Sun or light shade, drought-tolerant. ZONE 5 MIN, HARDY TO -28°C (-20°F).

Picea pungens 'Hillside'

A slow-growing spruce with grey-green needles. Growth is around 7–15cm (2 ¾–6in) per year, trees eventually forming a broad, dense, irregular, tear-drop shape. Sun. ZONE 3 MIN, HARDY TO -40°C (-40°F).

Muhlenbergia reverchonii

Relatively little-known, this is an unusual and attractive grass, growing to a maximum of 70cm (27 ½in), with a dense clump of fine basal foliage and delicate-looking glowing red flower/seed heads. Sun. ZONE 5 MIN, HARDY TO -26°C (-15°F).

Tom Stuart-Smith The Barn at Serge Hill, Hertfordshire, UK

TOM WAS brought up "150 yards down the road", and knows the stony, dry, hilltop soil intimately, and the lie of the land, which appears calmly rural, although only 30 minutes by train from central London. He now owns a small slice of the surrounding gently hilly, very English, landscape, and confesses that it is difficult to describe what is actually garden, but "probably about a couple of acres." Indeed, the distinction, separation and transition from garden to landscape dominates our conversation.

This garden reflects Tom's design style almost perfectly, although he says, "you always have to live with the zeitgeist of the past" – meaning that

design decisions made when you lay out a garden are very difficult to undo, and can end up defining it for life. Here, the bare bones were laid down in 1989, two years after Tom moved in, so he feels that the garden is slightly stuck in a time when British garden design was nothing like as open to new ideas as it became around ten years later. Firm axes of hornbeam hedges dominate, but much of the space is taken up with wide borders of expansive herbaceous planting. In many ways, this is the early 21st century take on the great herbaceous borders of Britain a century before, but with a plant palette heavily influenced by the Dutch- and German-led movements in planting

WITH ITS strong sense of plant architecture, Tom's garden looks back to the Arts and Crafts tradition that so dominated 20th century garden design in Britain, but the 'open borders' of perennials are firmly contemporary.

BIOGRAPHY Tom Stuart-Smith (born 1960) has become one of Britain's premier garden designers through doing what the British love best, gently tweaking tradition. His gardens seem to be genuinely rooted in history, but are, at the same time, unmistakeably contemporary.

Tom gardened as a child and, at the age of eighteen, met two of the greatest names in mid-20th century garden and landscape design, Lanning Roper and Geoffrey Jellicoe; "they were bursting with it, still in the prime of their working lives in their seventies," he remembers – they clearly made a big impact. A postgraduate degree in Landscape Architecture at Manchester University was followed by a job with a leading practice, Colvin and Moggridge. Here, he encountered Dutch ecological design, "Thijsse Park in Amstelveen made a huge impression[1]," he recalls. He then worked for Michael Brown, which mostly involved public housing projects, but as he says, "to be honest, I didn't want to be a social evangelist, my real skills were with private gardens... and then Penelope Hobhouse sent me a job she didn't have time to cope with, and that got me going." He then joined Elizabeth Banks Associates, working with them on one of their largest projects – the development of a new Royal Horticultural Society garden at Rosemoor in Devon. In 1998, with his first independent garden at the Chelsea Flower Show, Tom went completely freelance, but like many in the profession, he feels a bit lonely on his own. "I share a studio with two fellow designers, there are twelve people there now, there's so much life, I like being part of a group," he explains.

Since then, Tom has exhibited at Chelsea seven times, winning gold on each occasion. His commissions are almost all large country gardens, and stand firmly in the tradition that balances the creative tension of firm structure with bountiful, informal planting.

GARDENS OPEN TO THE PUBLIC

- **Broughton Grange** Oxfordshire, UK

- **Trentham Estate** Staffordshire, UK

- **Queen's Jubilee Garden at Windsor Castle** Berkshire, UK

- **Borders around the glasshouse at the Royal Horticultural Society Garden** Wisley, Surrey, UK

- **The Barn** Serge Hill, Hertfordshire, UK (occasionally through the National Gardens Scheme)

design; in late summer it is grasses and prairie perennials that dominate. In spring, scatterings of snowdrops, scillas and daffodils are followed by bold clumps of *Euphorbia palustris, camassias* and *aquilegias*. There is plenty of structure – not only the big hornbeam hedges, but also extensive lower ones of yew, cut in what has definitely become the fashion of the century's first decade, rhythmical rounded waves.

"I used to do nearly all the work in the garden myself," says Tom, which is impressive given the scale, "but then I hurt my back, and now employ a full-time gardener." This is obviously a regret, but there is the feeling that he keeps a very close eye on plant success and failure. Plant knowledge is crucial for the kind of botanically rich, British garden style Tom works with. The fact that this is

a dry site must be an advantage in gaining knowledge about what varieties to select for clients. He points out an inula, a yellow, daisy-flowered perennial, with impressively vast lower leaves, "that's 'Sonnenspeer', much the most drought-tolerant one", he says, "and phloxes, which I love, they vary enormously in how well they do on dry soils" – this is the kind of technical detail that can be very hard to find in nursery catalogues or reference books.

One area of the garden that has very definitely changed over time is the courtyard garden, defined by the three wings of the house (converted from agricultural buildings). "When we started we had all our vegetables here, and it got very cottagey, very Arts and Crafts, a bit too folksy," Tom says. In 2006, he rebuilt it, with

[1] The parks and roadsides of Amstelveen are famous for their naturalistic planting, mostly with native species. This suburb of Amsterdam has aimed at urban integration with nature since the 1930s.

W HERE ARE the paths?
One of the wonders
of big-scale perennial
planting is the apparent
disappearance of paths;
everything becomes a
dreamy herbaceous border
without boundaries.

rusted steel sheeting left over from a Chelsea garden, some minimal contemporary water features and a moodily effective mix of dark red astrantias, smaller grasses, sedum varieties, echinaceas and *Euphorbia* x *martini*. It is a highly effective combination of light textures, dark maroons, reds, pinks and greens.

With its hilltop location, you are never far from the view at Serge Hill. How the garden relates to the landscape is something that is clearly of great interest to Tom. Beyond the hedges on the north side is a great downhill sweep of wild flower meadow, sown about twenty years ago. There are loose clumps and scattered individual varieties of numerous tree species: maples, oaks, zelkovas, all of which would be read as natives by anyone at a greater distance of more than 100m (109yd). How the garden is seen from the outside is something that obviously causes some concern. "Gardens that spill out into the landscape can be a kind of pollution," he says. "Sue and I are debating about whether to hedge the garden in…

REPETITION always helps give a rhythm and unity to larger borders; here provided by violet *Nepeta* 'Six Hills Giant'. This is a design trick that is particularly useful in less formally structured plantings.

in the past I'd see the garden sitting in the landscape, but now, looking at it from outside, it looks rather curious from the other side of the valley, a bogus Brownian conceit. It seems more responsible to make sure that it is seen as just another compartment, so this year we are going to plant a hedge at the bottom of the meadow."

The soil is dry, and drought can clearly be an issue. "I grow things here that I shouldn't, such as eupatoriums, which require more moisture and need to be planted in a hole full of good compost," says Tom. "I'm not systematic in that way… and echinaceas too, I probably buy 50 every year (to replace losses)… the lovely thing about your own patch is that you can say 'Stuff the system, I'll do what I want.'" Clients' gardens in such a situation would have to be more rigorously based on species known to be drought-tolerant. But the right to be self-indulgent in plant selection is a weakness that nearly every other designer would recognise.

MOVING FURTHER away from the house, there is less herbaceous planting, big blocks of hedging with an almost megalithic quality dominate. Once surrounded by them, the gaze is very firmly directed along their axes.

SURROUNDED ON two sides by the house, this courtyard area is seen at all times of year and in all weathers. Not surprisingly, there is a long season of interest and most of the species used are relatively compact. Dark pinks (varieties of *Astrantia major*, later of *Echinacea purpurea*), and the yellow-greens of *Alchemilla mollis* and species of *Euphorbia* play an important role.

Some Favourite Plants

Asarum europaeum

A diminutive, evergreen ground cover for shade, with inconspicuous flowers and glossy, rounded, heart-shaped leaves – to no more than 15cm (6in). Slow-growing, but safe to use with bulbs and choice woodland plants. Moist, but well-drained soil. ZONE 4 MIN.

Eupatorium maculatum 'Riesenschirm'

Derived from one of the "Joe Pye weeds" of North America, this 2-m (6½-ft) high perennial giant of the border produces large heads of red-pink flowers in late summer, which are a magnet for butterflies. The sturdy stems, whilst not particularly decorative in themselves, stand the winter so well that they can be a valuable structural asset. Fertile, moisture-retentive soil in full sun. ZONE 4 MIN.

Euphorbia stygiana

The most patrician of several euphorbia species that are "evergreen without looking evergreen" – large, fresh green leaves with a prominent central midrib. A sub-shrub growing to little more than 80cm (31½in), it can sprawl to 1.5m (5ft). It has the usual greeny euphorbia flowers, with good honey scent in early spring. Shelter and good drainage are important. ZONE 8 MIN.

Hakonechloa macra

A grass whose broad fresh green leaves appear neatly combed, radiating out from a central clump. Growing to 60cm (23½in), it dies down completely in winter, so making a good plant to combine with early bulbs. The green form is considerably less readily available than the yellow 'Aureola', which Tom says he "cannot stand." Sun or light shade, moist but well-drained soil. ZONE 6 MIN.

Stipa calamagrostis (Achnatherum calamagrostis)

A delicate medium-sized (to 90cm/ 35in) grass with rich fawn flower/seed heads that complement lushly green foliage. Very graceful and combines well with smaller late-flowering perennials. Full sun, very drought-tolerant; indeed, on moister and richer soils it can flop badly (Tom conceals pea sticks in the plant early in the year to help hold it up). ZONE 5 MIN.

Zelkova serrata

"A well-grown one is a beautiful sight," says Tom, of a tree, distantly related to the elm, but fortunately not prone to the same diseases. Its graceful, spreading habit adds dignity to gardens where there is space for it. Coarsely toothed leaves that turn rich red in autumn and grey flaky bark. Best in deep, rich soils; tolerant of some shade. ZONE 5 MIN.

Joe Swift Joe's garden, London, UK

"I MADE IT totally for myself," says Joe of the 15 x 5m (49 x 16ft) garden he built in 2003 at the home in Hackney he had moved into with his wife and two children. "There was nothing there before, except a load of bindweed," so Joe was able to do just what he wanted, and to make a garden that has also proved very successful with the rest of the family. Most of the elements were very similar to the materials used in Modular Garden (see biography), "except for the pond – ponds need quite a bit of maintenance and understanding, so aren't good for a lot of people," he says. The hard materials might give the game away, and suggest that this is

another modular garden; the planting, however, is too personal, too eclectic to be anything but owner-designed.

Joe is known for his hatred of what was the heart of the traditional English garden, the lawn, so it is good to see that he practises what he preaches. "Lawns in small areas easily become barriers," he says. "If it is wet you can't go on it, and if the kids run on it they bring dirt into the house and ruin the grass." Decking is the best alternative, so Joe installed hardwood decking and Welsh slate. The slate was also used to build a retaining wall and to surround a raised level pond.

FURNISHING is weatherproof "although the cushions come in for the winter," says Joe. "I like to build furniture into gardens, though. There isn't enough comfy furniture for gardens around."

BIOGRAPHY Joe Swift (1965) is probably not the only designer in this book who must have been a bit of a worry to his parents as he was growing up. After dropping out of art college, he drifted into construction and the landscaping industry. A childhood of pottering about in gardens with his mother and grandparents had given him a feel for plant life, so a course at the English Gardening School seemed an obvious thing to do. "Having started off as a landscaper and builder, I was in a good position," he recalls, "as a lot of garden designers weren't confident with hard landscaping." He set up Plantroom, a garden design and build company in 1992, while his natural bonhomie and gift with words led him on to garden television programmes – he is now one of Britain's best-known presenters on *BBC GardenersWorld*.

Joe's most far-sighted move came in 2005, when he set up Modular Gardens with two partners, whose previous experience had been in the worlds of architecture, engineering and product design. The idea is to simplify the whole process of urban garden design, which should be "as easy as buying a car," he says, "or a new kitchen or bathroom... it's a bit like what Conran did with Habitat – making good design accessible." By now, many garden designers, whose motto since the 18th century has been "the genius of the place" (or *genius loci* if their public school education hasn't worn off), are squirming. But Joe makes a very good case for what some might call the IKEA-ization of the profession. "A lot of clients are not gardeners, they just want a space to enjoy, the classic outdoor room... lawns especially don't work in shade, or confined spaces... all too often gardens become frustrating spaces, a problem area... hard spaces

work." Potential clients are shown a laptop presentation of different gardens, plans and planting styles, all of which can be assembled from a limited, but carefully selected range of materials on which the company has negotiated good wholesale prices from suppliers. I was sceptical at first too, but Joe in the end convinced me.

Halfway down the garden there is a raised bed running the width of the garden, with a riot of mostly herbaceous colourful planting, and not immediately visible, a set of wooden steps that lead to an area where, as Joe describes, "I built a pergola-type structure out of scaffolding, it's the kid's area. They're twelve and ten now; they did have swings there when they were younger, and they climb up and chat to the neighbours' kids over the fence." The "pergola" is designed to be multi-use and to be able to serve different functions as time goes on; once the children have finally grown out of clambering on it, it can be used for climbers; it can also have a tarpaulin slung over it for shade.

Talking about his children, Joe says: "They use the garden a lot, they love the pond, and the

wildlife in there. But there is no room to play football, if they do that I tell them to go down the ****** park." He adds that there is no complete ban on boisterous play because the plants at the edges of the planting are "very robust and usually bounce back if accidentally hit." The slate in the garden has an additional function – "the kids both used to love chalking on the slate, drawing massive pictures."

The range of plants here is a very personal one, Joe explains: "I made a collection of all the plants I like, for height and interest... a lot of city gardens lack height... I try to bring plants as close to the house as possible. In a lot of gardens it's so bare around the house, but here you can sit and feel surrounded by plants." Joe says that he "tweaks the planting every year", and that

BIG PERENNIALS partially
screen a scaffolding
structure at the back of
the garden, designed for
multiple and constantly-
changing usage. The tall
yellow is *Verbascum
olympicum*, the red is
a *Helenium* variety.

he usually also grows a few herbs and tomatoes every summer. The planting is a mix of herbaceous and what could be called urban shrubby plants that benefit from the shelter and warmth of city gardens, such as the elegant evergreen *Euphorbia mellifera*, the majestic silver foliage of *Melianthus major* or *Polygala* x *dalmaisiana*, a small grey-leaved South African shrub with purple flowers, which Joe notes, "flowers on and on."

Having created the tools for so many city dwellers to enjoy their gardens, it is good to see that Joe clearly enjoys "his own medicine", and to see that a small garden can serve many functions. In particular, the mix of planting and hard surfaces encapsulates what he feels is appropriate in the city — "stone, brick and decking tie in the garden to the city landscape… an overly soft garden often just does not work, but other factors push planting, such as bio-diversity."

CREEPING *Acaena microphylla* (left) makes a good infill between decking steps, on their way to a raised pool. The grey is *Hebe pinguifolia* 'Sutherlandii'. (Above) A *Molinia caerulea* subsp. *arundinacea* 'Transparent' is just that, allowing you to see through it to plants behind. It develops fine pale yellow autumn colour.

Some Favourite Plants

Bidens heterophylla

A rare, but in Joe's words "quite aggressive" perennial member of the daisy family, with creamy-yellow flowers on leggy stems from mid-summer until early autumn. He reckons it "looks good with grasses, but warns that it does seed around". Damp soil in sun preferred – to 1.5m (5ft) tall.

Clerodendron bungei

An unusual, summer-flowering, suckering shrub with heads of deep pink flower, about which Joe says, "I love the name, everyone asks me what it is and I love telling them, but it can run." To 2.5m (8ft), with upright growth, suckering to form extensive patches. Likes sun and shelter. ZONE 8 MIN.

Hebe pinguifolia 'Sutherlandii'

"I've got a box phobia", says Joe; small-leaved hebes, however, can often fulfil the same function, especially since "this one doesn't need clipping". A low spreading shrub, with intense silvery grey, tiny, rounded leaves that hug densely-packed stems. It grows to 50cm (1¾ft) high and somewhat wider. Full sun is important to keep a tidy and dense shape. Wind and salt resistant and physically tough, but Joe reminds us that like most hebes "it doesn't last for ever". ZONE 7 MIN.

Miscanthus sinensis 'Silberfeder'

"This looks great backlit," says Joe. To get the best out of larger ornamental grasses, they need to be positioned carefully – so that late afternoon winter sunshine can strike the seed heads; a dark background helps as well. There are a great many varieties in cultivation, varying in colour and height. This one is tall, around 2m (6½ft), and silver-grey flower heads held well clear of the foliage. Full sun, but some light shade is also tolerated, average to moist soils. ZONE 4 MIN.

Molinia caerulea subsp. arundinacea 'Transparent'

"Great autumn colour, and I love the way it breaks off at the base and falls over, you just pick it up and chuck it on the compost heap," says Joe of this tough ornamental grass. All molinias have a "firework" habit – leaves and flower stems bursting forth from a tight clump, turning rich yellow or orange-brown shades in autumn, but then as Joe notes, disintegrating in early winter. Likes full sun, any soil except for the wettest, tolerant of low fertility. Potentially to 2m (6ft). ZONE 5 MIN.

Salix exigua Coyote Willow

This willow has "silvery, absolutely stunning" foliage, growing to 4m (13ft) high, with a shrubby, or sometimes more treelike habit. The leaves are elegantly narrow, the habit relatively upright, and slowly suckering – so in some ways rather bamboo-like. Dry to damp soils tolerated, full sun. ZONE 2 MIN.

Jacqueline van der Kloet, The Theetuin, Ueesp, Netherlands

THE THEETUIN IS, as might be expected, not just a place to come and look at plants, but to relax and be sociable too. Situated on an island in the River Vecht, inside the remains of a historic fortress, the green surroundings give no clue that this was once a military establishment; the building, which houses the tea room and Jacqueline's office, was once a munitions store!

Bulbs have conventionally been used in a very formulaic way; Jacqueline's mission is to integrate them into parks and gardens, alongside other plants, and preferably as permanent garden elements. At 1,200 sq m (0.3 acre), the garden is small enough to be intimate. The soil is heavy clay, which she has "tried to make lighter with compost and sand, but I never water, as plants should live without my helping them." Quite a lot of the garden is partially overshadowed by trees, so there are areas of dry shade. It is situations like this that make the Theetuin the kind of place to which many owners of small town gardens can relate. The atmosphere is intimate and homely, with firm structures created by hedges both external (beech) and internal (privet), and box clipped into a variety of shapes, including a peacock and a teddy bear – clipping has a very strong tradition in Holland.

"When we started," says Jacqueline, "we put in a lot of shrubs and began to shape them…

WHEN THIS picture was chosen for the book, Jacqueline joked that "raking gravel is the core business." She has always tried to do as much of the maintenance in the garden herself.

BIOGRAPHY "I do not work, I have a paid hobby, I live gardens, I sleep gardens. I will never retire... and I always can't wait to get back from holiday" – Jacqueline van der Kloet (born 1950) is passionate, even by the standards of a profession that tends to be particularly enthusiastic about its work. Originally trained as a landscape architect in Belgium, she worked at first with a practice in Amsterdam, which mainly designed and built public spaces. One job, however, was a private garden – "I discovered how much I enjoyed working on it," recalls Jacqueline. "It was more personal and involved more work with plant selection."

In 1983, Jacqueline opened her own office, and started designing private gardens full time. Around this time she made several trips to England, visiting some of the many private gardens that were open to the public; this gave her and a number of colleagues the idea to do something similar – so in 1986 they opened the Theetuin (tea garden), which combines a garden with a café. Initially, the garden was laid out with shrubs and perennials, but in 1994, the Netherlands-based International Flower Bulb Centre asked Jacqueline to trial some bulbs. She threw herself into combining bulbs with the other plants she used, the results were good, word spread and she soon acquired a strong national reputation for her planting combinations.

Jacqueline's career has come full circle, as her work now is almost entirely designing plantings in public spaces, creating combinations of bulbs for a succession of flowering plants, amalgamated with annuals and perennials. These are made for a variety of both permanent and temporary plantings, including Keukenhof, a park near Amsterdam, famous for its dramatic displays of bulbs in spring, and for the Floriades (major festivals of Dutch horticulture, held every ten years). She has also worked with Piet Oudolf on the Lurie Garden in Chicago, and Battery Park in New York City.

Bulbs, tulips in particular, have long suffered a reputation for being used in an unsubtle way, planted en masse for knockout value. Jacqueline is leading a movement to use them as seasonal elements in a more holistic way. Her technique is to scatter and intermingle them, and other plants, in a naturalistic way – "I like the description of my work as milleflore or confetti," she says.

structure is so important in winter." In the centre of the garden is an oval enclosed area, defined by a cypress hedge ("a present from a nurseryman we worked a lot with, so we couldn't say no"), inside which is a brick-edged pool. Jacqueline explains the rationale: "There needed to be an element in the centre of the garden which meant you couldn't see the whole in one go. It is a central meditational area, a place of calm and quiet."

In many ways this is an experimental garden, a place for people to come and look at different garden situations, such as sunny and dry shady areas, to be inspired, but in particular to see what works, especially combinations involving bulbs. "Bulbs have a reputation for having loud colours," says Jacqueline, "so I show people what I do here, that bulbs can look good alongside other plants." Trialling new plants is important, as she explains: "I don't like to use plants in my professional work without having tried them myself... there are new tulips all the time, many new alliums, also some completely new genera, such as *Bellevalia*, they are like *Muscari*."

THE CENTRE of the garden is a dark pool surrounded by a cypress hedge, openings in which offer enticing views out (left). The blue is *Iris sibirica* 'Caesar'. The 'tree' whose trunks dominate the picture is *Aralia cordata* – in fact a upright suckering shrub with elegantly grand foliage.

TULIP 'Jimmy' amongst pale yellow Oxlips (*Primula elatior*) and the dark red leaves of *Euphorbia dulcis* 'Chameleon'. Red or bronze foliage is often a good foil for the colours of bulbs.

Jacqueline has a particular interest in identifying and encouraging bulbs that reliably flower year after year, and the Theetuin is a good place to observe these, and the conditions that promote this most useful (and sustainable) habit. "The period after flowering is particularly important," she notes. "There should be at least six weeks when the foliage should not be shaded, good drainage is also important." Central to her work is the integration of bulbs with other plants, and her experience here is that "nearly all perennials, except for the very invasive ones, can be easily combined with bulbs." After the bulbs have finished, there is still plenty to admire here – during the summer hydrangeas and Japanese anemones make a colourful impact. The fact that much of the garden is under at least some thirsty tree canopy makes the selection of drought- and

MAGENTA *Geranium psilostemon* is a first-class perennial for mid-summer flower, in sun or light shade. Here it is joined by pale pink *Papaver* 'Helen Elizabeth'. The geranium has foliage that is expansive enough to cover ground now vacated by the bulbs.

shade-tolerant species vital; plants, however, must not be so competitive that they suppress bulb foliage – *Geranium macrorrhizum*, liriope and hellebore have proved successful.

"For many years," says Jacqueline, "I did all the maintenance myself, but then in 2006, in May, it all got too much for me, so now I have a lady who comes in when I need her… but I still do a lot myself."

She also says, "I like to see how the garden develops without my interfering." In other words, plants are allowed to spread, jostle for position and find their own balance to a large extent. Combining a relaxed feeling with the clipped order characteristic of Dutch gardens, this is a garden packed full of interest, but one that many owners of small gardens could learn a lot from – over a cup of tea and piece of cake.

Views vary on clipping, but in Holland and Belgium it is seen as a central part of garden art. In long, and sometimes dull, winters, green structure is particularly welcomed.

Some Favourite Plants

Anemone x hybrida 'Honorine Jobert'

A mid- to late-summer flowering perennial that Jacqueline loves for the purity of its white flowers, which do a particularly good job of bringing light to shady corners – to 1.5m (5ft), and slowly spreading to form large clumps. Easy, vigorous and reliable – although, like all of these big anemones, it can be slow to establish. Full sun (but only if drought is not a problem), or light shade; fertile soils preferred. ZONE 6 MIN.

Crocosmia 'George Davison'

The "montbretias" are bulbous perennials that vary greatly in hardiness. Not all are hardy in Holland, but this is one of the tougher ones, with clear yellow, star-shaped flowers on 90cm (3ft) stems. Fresh green linear leaves add a distinct note to the border even before the plant starts flowering in late summer. Full sun, moist but well-drained soils. ZONE 7 MIN.

Dahlia 'North Star'

This new dahlia hybrid is single with a clear starlike outline – and a better, stronger scent than dahlias are known for. Dahlias are enjoying a revival in fashion, as gardeners recognise just how useful they are for injecting late season colour into a border. Unless the area has very mild winters, they are best dug up at the end of the season and the tubers stored in a dry place until re-planting time again next spring. Full sun and fertile soil needed for best results.

Deinanthe caerulea

Related to the hydrangea, the deinanthes are a group of rarely seen woodland perennials of singular beauty. The leaves are relatively large, with a deep notch at the tip, the flowers, produced in early summer, are rounded, fleshy and pale blue in colour – like exquisitely hand-crafted buttons – to 60cm(2ft) high. Shade and moist, but well-drained, humus-rich soil is essential. ZONE 4 MIN.

Narcissus 'Ice Wings'

Jacqueline says "this is a more elegant version of 'Thalia'" – a popular and old established triandrus variety, where the "petals" are slightly swept back and the central cup is prominent and rounded. Like 'Thalia' the flowers are ivory-white. To 30cm (12in) high, early spring flowering. Sun or light shade. ZONE 5 MIN.

Tulipa 'Violet Beauty'

This is a tulip with a classic goblet shape, and pinkish soft violet blooms, perfect for combining with pink or white flowers – to 40cm (15½in) high. This is a particularly sturdy variety, suitable for both the border and containers. Flowering late spring.

James van Sweden Chesapeake Bay, USA

"I WANT IT to be ugly" is not something that one often hears garden owners saying, but then James van Sweden has made something of a career out of being iconoclastic. For many years James's personal gardening was limited to a tiny plot in Georgetown, Washington, DC, but in 1998 he bought a property on the shoreline of Chesapeake Bay – a place that had been for sale for 11 years, as nobody else wanted it. James commissioned the architect Suman Sorg (known for her work designing American embassies) to create a house that incorporated as many views of the adjacent countryside as possible.

The surroundings are flat and pared-down almost to being minimal, and dominated by Chesapeake Bay – indeed, the land hardly feels any higher than the water. Some might think that the place is bleak, but James was drawn to its openness and simplicity. "I love it," he says, "I love the flatness of the landscape… the big view… hills get in the way of a good view… it's like Holland, my ancestral country." In winter, in clear sunny weather, it feels almost bleached: yellow or brown grass, grey trees, the only colour being the odd evergreen and the intense blue of the sky. It is certainly not a place for a conventional garden.

"I wanted a tough garden, not a pretty pretty one," says James, "with no lawn, and meadow

DECKING IS perfect for a flat environment, as the smallest elevation can make a lot of difference to views, especially when there is any kind of wildflower or grass planting involved too.

BIOGRAPHY Future generations will remember the remarkable business partnership of James van Sweden (1935) and Wolfgang Oehme (1930) as marking a turning point in the history of landscape design in the USA. Oehme van Sweden Associates challenged the supremacy of the lawn and the heavy hand of the evergreen. Starting with private gardens in the 1970s, they moved on to public landscapes, with a highly acclaimed garden for the Federal Reserve Bank in Washington, DC, in 1977. Initially, they were very controversial, as they used herbaceous perennials and grasses – plants that bank employees thought were weeds. Whilst much of the practice's work is corporate or public, residential gardens represent the real heart of the business. It is in private gardens that a real diversity of plants can be used, and complex relationships built up between them; there is scope for innovation, too.

The success of Oehme van Sweden Associates has a great deal to do with the very different skills and character of the two men: James trained as an architect and is basically concerned with spatial design, Wolfgang trained as a horticulturalist in eastern Germany in the 1950s. James is outgoing and a born businessman, Wolfgang is obsessive about, and highly focused on, his plants. Brought up in Michigan, on the edge of the prairies, James has always loved the sparse beauty of grasses, but it was Wolfgang who saw their potential as garden or landscape plants. A key figure in horticulture and planting design during Wolfgang's formative years in Germany was Karl Foerster (1874–1970), who had pioneered the use of ornamental grasses and other "non-conventional" garden plants. The company has continued to expand, and is now increasingly run by younger partners brought into the company by James. Commissions are now likely to come from all over the USA, and from abroad.

The practice's signature planting is of large ornamental grasses and drifts of perennials, which to many eyes looks wild enough to evoke natural grassland. In fact, Oehme van Sweden plantings are generally highly structured – the wild look being more apparent than real. In recent years, they have begun to alter the way in which plants are combined, working more with intermingling species and using native plants, particularly where a project includes an existing, bio-diverse, semi-natural landscape.

Writing and lecturing have always featured heavily in James's and Wolfgang's work – part of their mission is not just to design gardens and landscapes but to influence others and to educate. They have perhaps done more than anyone else in the USA to encourage private gardeners to use herbaceous plants in domestic landscapes.

GARDENS AND PARKS OPEN TO THE PUBLIC

- **Garden of the Federal Reserve Bank** Washington, DC

- **German American Friendship Garden** Washington, DC

- **Rockefeller Park** Battery Park City, New York City

- **Gardens of the Great Basin** Chicago Botanic Garden

- **North Point Park** Boston

right up to the house." The majority of the plants used are natives, with an emphasis on large perennials and grasses, and resilient trees and shrubs; as James puts it, "I like coarse, sculptural, aggressive plants." Physical toughness is a useful characteristic next to the coast in any case, whilst plants that are visually robust are needed simply to be appreciated in such a landscape. The artistically rough-and-ready look of the house and the garden is continued by the use of driftwood for garden seats, a fence and a small "folly", on a platform by the water's edge.

The site was little more than abandoned farmland, which a variety of native plants had begun to recolonise. James decided to preserve

large areas of these old fields, a total of 2.8 hectares (7 acres), one area between the house and waterside, and another swathe stretching out on the southern side of the property. Leading native plant specialist Darrel Morrison was brought in to advise on the fields; his opinion was that the old fields should simply be left, cutting only once a year to discourage woody plant regeneration. The result is a meadow dominated by two very striking grasses: *Schizachrium scoparium* (Little bluestem), which develops a rich bronze-brown colour in the autumn, and which is a dominant element in the local landscape until spring; and *Panicum virgatum* (Switch grass). Both these native species are used in borders around the house, and indeed

THE GUEST house. Native grass *Schizachrium scoparium* is part of the garden but grades into a wild grass community where it is one component amongst many. It is potentially a highly decorative species, especially since plant-hunting nursery owners have now turned up some very good forms for gardens, often with distinctly coloured foliage.

cultivars have become well-established in the nursery trade. As with any other area of "waste" land in the eastern USA, native asters and goldenrods have established themselves, too.

The planted area around the house incorporates a variety of perennials, whose wild character makes for a seamless transition with the meadow. Those who are used to nicely restrained perennials that sit politely in borders may be in for a shock; the sheer size of many of the plants is impressive, and clearly thrills James. "The *silphiums* are nine foot [2.7m], *Rudbeckia maxima* seven or eight foot [2 or 2.5m]," he states enthusiastically. Both are prairie plants belonging

to the daisy family: *Silphium perfoliatum* has yellow flowers, large deep green leaves and something of the build of a vegetable Rambo, while the rudbeckia is a more elegant plant with yellow petals reflexed back from a prominent central dark cone and large blue-grey basal leaves.

"It changes dramatically, every week is different," James says. "It works well as an all-season garden, it's especially good in winter, and I don't cut it down until February." Spring, here, starts with the fresh green shoots of grasses and perennials, but also with flowering trees and shrubs. It is these, perhaps, that have made the biggest impact on the landscape since James

started the garden, with a pine hedge along the northern side of the property, which is extensively boosted with various, mostly native, species. There are viburnums, *amelanchier*, *Hydrangea quercifolia* and several magnolias. Further tree planting has been used to screen the house from a nearby lane, and there is a pond between these trees and a small guest house, reached from the main house via decking. Building the garden was handled very much as many of the practice's commercial projects were – James designed the broad outline and Wolfgang filled this in with planting. "We did it together… we had a lot of fun," James records, "and I have learnt a lot.

I have tried to avoid the quilted look we've done in a lot of our work. Some things we have planted to look like they have self-sown, and I don't pull out the silphium seedlings. I'm tired of the quilt. Now I want the look of the one that got away."

In this area, with little human population, wildlife abounds and sees no barrier between nature and garden. "Deer come right up to the house," James reports, "but it's not a problem, as they have plenty to eat around the property, and I love the goldfinches on the rudbeckia." On one visit I was thrilled to be able to sit in the living room and watch ospreys feed their chicks in a nest at the shoreline.

THE VIEW from the shore – a sea of wild grasses on abandoned arable land provides a simple surround for a building style that James likes to call "unresolved". The wild grasses help blur the obvious boundaries of the property, even to obscure the fact that this is a house at all. This is important in a landscape of such simplicity and openness as this.

Some Favourite Plants

Symphyotrichum oblongifolium '**October Skies**' aromatic aster

One of many North American native asters, this particular variety shows great promise as ground cover, as it forms a low mound to a maximum height of around 40cm (16in). It is smothered with dark lavender daisies in autumn. Most soils, with some drought tolerance. ZONE 3 MIN.

Celtis occidentalis hackberry

"According to most people," says James, "this tree has no value whatsoever, but I love it, it has a sense of humour, it grows in a higgledy-piggledy way in every direction." Importantly, it is a robust native-American, shade tree, which, when grown in the open, develops a broad and expansive canopy. Potentially can grow to 30m (100ft). It is very tolerant of soil and site/position. ZONE 3 MIN.

Panicum virgatum '**Cloud Nine**' switch grass

This important prairie grass has become one of the most planted ornamental species. Growing to around 2m (6½ft), with a 1m (3ft 3in) spread, it makes a major impact from late summer to winter with a cloudlike head of tiny flowers, followed by seed. This particular selection is silver-grey in tone. Likes full sun and fertile soil. ZONE 4 MIN.

Pycnanthemum virginianum
mountain mint

"This plant looks so cool in the summer," says James. This species has white or pale lavender flowers atop 1m (3ft) high, tidy, bushy-looking plants, which James says "looks almost like boxwood, they are so dense." Bees love it, and the minty smell is very distinctive. Sun or light shade, average to damp soils. ZONE 3 MIN.

Schizachyrium scoparium
little blue stem

This grass that is very common across the USA and southern Canada, brings tones of silver-grey and red-pink to roadsides, prairie and wasteland. It has great potential as a garden plant – several superior strains are now available commercially. Height to 90cm (3ft) in garden conditions; any soil in full sun. ZONE 3 MIN.

Tradescantia x andersoniana 'Concord Grape'

A relatively new cultivar, the rich purple flowers and grey-toned leaves of this long-flowering summer perennial have won over many gardeners and designers. Generally happy in a wide range of conditions, it actually prefers moister ones; full sun or partial shade. Height to 40cm (16 in). ZONE 4 MIN.

Cleve West West London, UK

CLEVE'S GARDEN is a very typical urban plot, 12m (40ft) long and 4.5m (15ft) wide, on the south side of a 1960s house in the outer suburbs of west London. He made the garden in 1994 as a show garden that could be photographed for promotional purposes. He says that he "spends only a couple of days a year working in it – the main task is clipping the ivy." It is the ivy which really makes this garden; it covers all three fences – several different varieties mixed in together; the effect is of a green wall at just above head height (2m/6½ft), so that you are almost unaware of neighbouring houses or gardens. It feels like a very secret, very lush, little oasis.

A path of York stone runs down the central axis, but after a few metres from the house you have to step over a small pool on a stepping stone, and then over what Cleve calls the "tadpole maze", an ingenious extension to the pool where paving setts are set at around 2cm (¾in) apart, with the water of the pool flowing around them (and an accompanying layer of bright green, floating duckweed). The water is kept at just below the level of the walking surface. Beyond this is a small shed, with a roof that carries on over the path to form a gateway, dividing the garden in half. The roof was grassed, but drought killed the grass, so it is now planted with drought-tolerant sedum.

CLEVE has worked with sculptor Johnny Woodford on several garden projects. His spiky, chunky style is at home amongst the sculptural foliage which is a particular love of Cleve's.

Cleve West (born 1958) is perhaps best known for the show gardens he has designed for the Chelsea Flower Show and for the Hampton Court Palace Flower Show – the first (for Hampton Court) was in 1994. "I've built quite a career out of show gardens," he says. "They don't necessarily help you get business and they stop you doing lot of other things, but if you are paid for doing them, it's worthwhile." Obtaining the plants (which always involves allowing for a huge level of contingency), materials and labour requires great organisational skills, clear focus and stamina. Perhaps Cleve's first career as a track and field athlete, specialising in the long jump, was a good training for building show gardens.

After his athletic career came to its inevitable end, Cleve started working for a fine art publisher. At one stage, this involved spending a week with David Hockney in his studio, which Cleve describes as "a wonderful experience". Around this time, he started to help an elderly aunt in London keep on top of her garden, and discovered that he really enjoyed the work. In 1990, Cleve did a John Brookes design course – "John is a brilliant teacher, you really feel like you are getting a grip," he recalls. He went on to start working in gardens, maintenance at first, then design and build, and finally design only. As he explains: "You have to give up the building as your body gets older, but you miss something. When you are actually constructing a garden, you can see opportunities to develop things that happen by chance, which you are removed from if you are only designing... when I'm building, I never stick to a plan."

Cleve's early gardens often involved collaboration between himself and an artist – for instance, Johnny Woodford. "Very spiky stuff," he remembers, "either as contrast with softer planting or to keep up with plants like yuccas... I'm still interested in sculpture but it can just as easily be trees or plants... I have to find sculpture I like, but then it's usually very expensive".

Cleve's work is almost entirely residential, both urban and rural gardens. He has worked for clients in Normandy, France, which he enjoys, as "there are more traditional craftspeople, so it's a lot easier if you need sculpture fabricated than in England." He sees himself working in a way that balances "bold structures and looser forms".

There is more ivy crawling up some of it, and on the rear, at one side, a mass of *Muehlenbeckia complexa*, a climber of New Zealand origin which forms a tangled mass of thin, dark, wiry stems and tiny round leaves.

Planting spaces are limited to areas at the side of the shed, and a number of raised beds, with retaining walls made of paving setts, around the edges. Much of the planting emphasises the defining lush green feel. There are ferns, some clipped box, and a variety of quite sculptural plants in pots hanging around. "The garden does

become something of a holding bay for plants," Cleve confesses. "I'm a bit of a magpie in nurseries, I buy plants for myself but know that I won't actually use them, and after a while they'll end up in a favourite client's garden." The clipped box in the centre of the garden was planted around the base of a big pear tree that once stood here and was a major feature; it died suddenly from fire blight and Cleve still feels its loss keenly. It has been replaced by a small specimen of *Stewartia sinensis*, so that it can develop its own character, and adapt to the given space and light

THE step-over pond (left) with the 'tadpole maze' on the far side. The structure in the centre is a combined archway and shed, with a grass roof. Seats, also by Johnny Woodford, resemble giant seeds until they are opened up.
(Above) Another Woodford sculpture drips water over wooden balls. Over time it has slowly begun to decay – Cleve says that he sees this bio-degradation as part of the interest of the piece.

1 "Allotments" are a great British tradition, rented plots of land, roughly equivalent to the community gardens of the US. They were mostly established in the late 19th century, to enable working people in terraced houses to grow their own vegetables.

Allotments have always had an air of the temporary and make-do. Cleve and Christine's subtle artistic interventions fit in well with this, encouraging the onlooker to look twice and question what they are seeing. Some sculptural material can also serve a function – supporting netting to defend crops from cabbage white butterflies.

conditions as it grows. Just by the door from the house to the garden is a massive round concrete table, given to him by the artists who had supplied some sculpture for a show garden, and a number of contemporary-looking steel chairs. Its chunky quality might overwhelm many a small garden, but here it is a good complement to the preponderant feeling of green. There are a number of wooden sculptures, now rotting away, and home to woodworm, woodlice and toads; Cleve had considered replacing them but in the end felt that they should stay and slowly biodegrade – "I love the feeling of decay, and the sense that gardens are never the same."

The allotment

There is not much space to actually garden at home, so Cleve and his partner Christine also have an allotment[1], about a ten-minute cycle-ride away, where he says, "we manage to grow most vegetables... we got it in 1999, it was about having some space to garden in as much as a source of vegetables. In fact, we've got four small allotments, so are entitled to four sheds ...we have a few ornamentals too, like *Verbena bonariensis* and nigella for the bees. We've even got a couple of self-seeded oaks themselves, maybe not a good idea, but we're trying to pollard them." There are plenty of artistically displayed found objects around. "We have a Derek Jarman type atmosphere," says Cleve. There are also some more self-consciously sculptural creations such as an old chain wrapped around a wigwam of sticks.

Cleve explains, "Having the allotment is as much about meeting friends and the social thing as anything... it's a very lively place, not always peaceful as we get our fair share of disputes and stealing but, on the whole, it is an enriching place and it keeps us healthy." So much goes on here that Cleve says, "I've co-written a sit-com based on the allotment, there is so much material."

Some Favourite Plants

Acanthus hungaricus

A more refined version of the familiar *Acanthus mollis*. Vast leaves to 1m (3ft) long are deeply divided, and produced early in the year, followed in summer by grand 1.5m (5ft) tall spikes of chunky, pale pink flowers, with dusky purple hoods. The seed heads stand well and are a good early winter feature. In warm climates it may go dormant in mid-summer, to re-emerge in autumn. Sun or, in warm climates, shade, and fertile soil. ZONE 7 MIN.

Hedera hibernica, Iris Ivy

"It sounds boring but I like to use ivy as ground cover," says Cleve. Ivy thrives in the dry shade below trees where nearly all-else fails. This species is the one most commonly planted – for its unobtrusive broad foliage and ease of growth. Eventual height 7m (23ft), but as a ground cover spread is infinite. Slow growth in the initial stages means planting at 40cm (16in) intervals is advisable. *Hedera* species are regarded as dangerously invasive in western North America. ZONE 7 MIN.

Hydrangea aspera

A hydrangea worth growing for its magnificent foliage as much as its mid-summer borne, flat heads of tiny, mauve flowers, surrounded by large white sterile bracts; the leaves are up to 20cm (8in) long, broad and covered in coarse hairs. Growing to 3.5m (11ft), it slowly suckers to form clumps. Best in well-drained moist soils in light shade. ZONE 7 MIN.

Polysticum setiferum

"I am drawn to ferns, I used to live on Exmoor, which has wonderful ferns growing around the waterfalls," recalls Cleve. "They are also useful in a slug-infested garden." This species is one that is particularly widely grown, as it is somewhat more drought and sun tolerant than most. The foliage is also finely and elegantly divided – 60cm (24in), height and width. Best in light shade and moist, but well-drained soils. Evergreen in milder climates. ZONE 6 MIN.

Miscanthus nepalensis

A particularly fine species of ornamental grass, closely related to the familiar *M. sinensis*, although considerably less hardy. Pendant, golden-tinged, 1–1.5-m (3–5-ft) high flower heads in late summer held well above a neat tuft of soft green foliage. Any good soil in full sun. ZONE 8 MIN.

Stewartia sinensis

Stewartias are rather splendid relatives of the camellia, but only rarely seen. This one is a large shrub or small tree, with attractive cinnamon-coloured, flaking bark, fragrant white flowers in early summer and rich crimson autumn colour. Deep, moist, but well-drained, acidic soils and shelter from wind are necessary for success. ZONE 5 MIN.

Contact details

Private gardens are open only if details are given here.

James Alexander Sinclair
www.blackpitts.co.uk

Julian & Isabel Bannerman
www.bannermandesign.com
Hanham Court, Gloucestershire is open regularly during the summer (see website), also occasionally for NGS.

Susan Berger
Has now retired.

John Brookes
www.denmans-garden.co.uk
Denmans, Sussex is open regularly (see website), also occasionally for NGS.

Roberto Burle Marx Studio
www.burlemarx.com.br/ingles.htm
The Burle Marx garden is now owned by the Brazilian government and run as a national monument; it is possible to visit the garden.
Sítio Roberto Burle Marx
Estrada Burle Max de Guaratiba, 2019
Rio de Janeiro 23020-240 Brazil
+55 21 2410 1412/ 2410-1171
Opening: Tours: 9:30am & 1:30pm Mon-Sun by appointment only.

Tracy DiSabato Aust
www.tracylive.com

Christine Facer
www.christinefacer.com
Open by appointment only for groups of 20 or more from May to September.

Nancy Goslee Power
www.nancypower.com

Naila Green
www.nailagreengardendesign.co.uk

Isabelle Greene
www.isabellegreene.com

Penelope Hobhouse
Has now retired.

Raymond Jungles
www.raymondjungles.com

Noel Kingsbury
www.noelkingsbury.com

Jantiene T. Klein Roseboom
www.imaginationdesign.com

Arabella Lennox-Boyd
www.arabellalennoxboyd.com
Gresgarth Hall, Lancashire, has regular openings through the summer (see website).

Katie Lukas
www.stonehousegarden.co.uk
Stone House garden, Gloucestershire is open by appointment (see website), and occasionally for NGS.

Ulf Nordfjell
www.nordfjellcollection.se

Christine Orel
www.orel-plus-heidrich.de

Piet Oudolf
www.oudolf.com
The garden at Hummelo is open during nursery open hours (see www.oudolf.com/anja-oudolf/openingstijden for details).

Mien Ruys Studio

www.mienruys.nl
The Mien Ruys Garden at Dedemsvaart, is open regularly
(see www.mienruys.nl/tuinen for details).

Lauren Springer Ogden & Scott Ogden

www.plantdrivendesign.com

Tom Stuart-Smith

www.tomstuartsmith.co.uk
The garden at Serge Hill is open occasionally for the NGS.

Joe Swift

www.joeswift.co.uk

Jacqueline van der Kloet, NL

www.theetuin.nl
The Theetuin is regularly open (see website).

James van Sweden

www.ovsla.com

Cleve West

www.clevewest.com

NGS – The (UK) National Gardens Scheme

www.ngs.org.uk

Further reading

Publishers are given for the most recent edition in the originating country; publisher details may be different in other countries and older editions.

James Alexander-Sinclair
"Gardeners' World" 101 – Bold and Beautiful Flowers: For Year-round Colour
BBC Books, 2008

Close, A Journey In Scotland
(with Allan Pollok-Morris and others)
Northfield Print, 2008

Sue Berger
Allotment Gardening: An Organic Guide for Beginners
Green Books, 2005

John Brookes
Garden Planning Pocket Encyclopedia
Dorling Kindersley, 1999

The New Garden
Dorling Kindersley, 2002

Garden Design
Dorling Kindersley, 2001

Garden Masterclass
Dorling Kindersley, 2002

Small Garden
Dorling Kindersley, 2006

Garden Design Course
Mitchell Beazley, 2007

Well-designed garden
Dorling Kindersley, 2007

Room Outside
GardenArt Press, 2007

Tracy DiSabato Aust
The Well-Tended Perennial Garden: Planting and Pruning Techniques
Timber Press, 2006

50 High-Impact, Low-Care Garden Plants
Timber Press, 2009

The Well-Designed Mixed Garden: Building Beds and Borders with Trees, Shrubs, Perennials, Annuals, and Bulbs
Timber Press, 2009

Nancy Goslee Power
The Gardens of California: Four Centuries of Design from Mission to Modern
(with Susan Heeger and Michael Hales)
Hennessey & Ingalls, 2001

Power of Gardens
Stewart, Tabori & Chang, 2009

Penelope Hobhouse
(A selection)
Garden Style
Frances Lincoln, 2008

Plants in Garden History
Pavilion, 1992 (published by Simon & Schuster, New York as *Gardening Through the Ages*)

Penelope Hobhouse on Gardening
Frances Lincoln, 1994

Penelope Hobhouse's Garden Designs
Frances Lincoln, 1997

Penelope Hobhouse's Natural Planting
Pavilion, 1997

A Gardeners Journal
Frances Lincoln 1997

Gardens of Italy A Touring Guide
Mitchell Beazley, 1988

Colour In Your Garden
Collins, 1985

Raymond Jungles
The Colors of Nature, Subtropical Gardens
Monacelli Press, 2008

Noel Kingsbury
(a selection)
The New Perennial Garden
Frances Lincoln, 1996

Planting Green Roofs and Living Walls
(with Nigel Dunnett)
Timber Press, 2008

VISTA: the culture and politics of the garden (co-edited with Tim Richardson)
Frances Lincoln, 2005

Seedheads
Timber Press, 2006

Natural Garden Style
Merrell, 2009

Hybrid – The History and Science of Plant Breeding
University of Chicago Press, 2009

Arabella Lennox-Boyd

Designing Gardens
Frances Lincoln, 2002

Traditional English Gardens
Weidenfeld & Nicolson, 1988

Private gardens of London
Weidenfeld & Nicolson, 1990

Ulf Nordfjell

Ulf Nordfjell: Fourteen Gardens
Frances Lincoln, 2010

Lauren Springer Ogden and Scott Ogden

Plant-Driven Design: Creating Gardens That Honor Plants, Place, and Spirit
Timber Press, 2009

Lauren Springer

Passionate Gardening: Good Advice for Challenging Climates
(with Rob Proctor)
Fulcrum Publishing 2000

The Undaunted Garden: Planting for Weather-Resilient Beauty
Fulcrum Publishing 2000

Scott Ogden

Garden Bulbs for the South
Timber Press, 2007

Gardening Success with Difficult Soils: Limestone, Alkaline Clay, and Caliche Soils
Taylor Trade Publishing, 1992

The Moonlit Garden
Taylor Trade Publishing, 1998

Christine Orel

Der neue Blumen- und Staudengarten
Ulmer 2004

Piet Oudolf

Designing with Plants
(with Noel Kingsbury)
Timber Press, 2009

Planting Design: Gardens in Time and Space (with Noel Kingsbury)
Timber Press, 2005

Dream Plants for the Natural Garden
(with Henk Gerritsen)
Timber Press, 2000

Planting the Natural Garden
(with Henk Gerritsen)
Timber Press, 2003

Gardening with Grasses
(with Michael King)
Timber Press, 1998

Joe Swift

The Plant Room
BBC Books, 2001

Joe's Urban Garden Handbook
Quadrille, 2008

Joe's Allotment
BBC Books, April 2009

James van Sweden

The Arts and the Garden
Random House, 2007

Architecture in the Garden
Random House, 2002

Gardening with Nature
Watson-Guptill Publications and Grayson Publishing, 2003

Gardening with Water
Watson-Guptill Publications and Grayson Publishing, 2003

Bold Romantic Gardens: The New World Landscapes of Oehme and van Sweden (with Wolfgang Oehme)
Spacemaker Press, 1998

Index

Picture credits

6–10 Noel Kingsbury; 12–13 Andrea Jones / Garden Exposures Photo Library / Design: James Alexander-Sinclair; 14–17 James Alexander-Sinclair; 18 left GAP Photos / J S Sira; 18 centre James Alexander-Sinclair; 18 right Fotolia / KIM PHOTOS; 19 left Fotolia / Colette; 19 centre GAP Photos / John Glover; 19 right GAP Photos / Dianna Jazwinski; 20 Photograph Andrew Lawson / Designers: Isabel & Julian Bannerman; 21 Photograph Andrew Lawson; 22–27 Photograph Andrew Lawson / Designers: Isabel & Julian Bannerman; 28 left GAP Photos / Christina Bollen; 28 centre GAP Photos / Zara Napier; 28 right GAP Photos / Mark Bolton; 29 left GAP Photos / John Glover; 29 centre GAP Photos / Zara Napier; 29 right GAP Photos / Richard Bloom; 30–35 Photos: Huntley Hedworth / Garden design: Sue Berger; 36 left GAP Photos / Mark Bolton; 36 centre GAP Photos / Rob Whitworth; 36 right GAP Photos / J S Sira; 37 left GAP Photos / Lynn Keddie; 37 centre GAP Photos / Kit Young; 37 right GAP Photos / Martin Hughes-Jones; 38 Andrea Jones / Garden Exposures Photo Library / Design: John Brookes; 39 John Brookes; 40–41 Andrea Jones / Garden Exposures Photo Library / Design: John Brookes; 42–43 MMGI / Marianne Majerus / Denmans Gardens, Sussex / John Brookes; 44 left GAP Photos / Clive Nichols; 44 right GAP Photos / Gerald Majumdar; 45 left GAP Photos / Martin Hughes-Jones; 45 centre GAP Photos / John Glover; 45 right GAP Photos / Mark Bolton; 46 Andrea Jones / Garden Exposures Photo Library / Design: Roberto Burle-Marx (Burle-Marx & Cia. Ltda); 47 Corbis / Farrell Grehan; 48–51 Andrea Jones / Garden Exposures Photo Library / Design: Roberto Burle-Marx (Burle-Marx & Cia. Ltda); 52 left GAP Photos / Andrea Jones; 52 centre The Garden Collection / GWI / G Delacroix; 52 right GAP Photos / Andrea Jones; 53 left GAP Photos / J S Sira; 53 centre GAP Photos / John Glover; 53 right GAP Photos / FhF Greenmedia; 54–57 Ian Adams; 58–59 Tracy DiSabato Aust; 60 left GAP Photos / FhF Greenmedia; 60 centre GAP Photos / Jonathan Buckley; 60 right GAP Photos / Neil Holmes; 61 left GAP Photos / Adrian Bloom; 61 centre GAP Photos / John Glover; 61 right GAP Photos / Heather Edwards; 62–67 Christine Facer; 68 left GAP Photos / Richard Bloom; 68 centre GAP Photos / Paul Debois; 68 right GAP Photos / Marcus Harpur; 69 left GAP Photos / Rob Whitworth; 69 centre & right Christine Facer; 70 Marcia Lee; 71 Victoria Pearson; 72–73 Marcia Lee; 74 left Tim Street-Porter; 74 centre GAP Photos / Martin Hughes-Jones; 74 right–75 left Marcia Lee; 75 centre and right Nancy Goslee Power; 76 Andrea Jones / Garden Exposures Photo Library / Design: Naila Green Garden Design; 77 Photography: Ian Green; 78–81 Andrea Jones / Garden Exposures Photo Library / Design: Naila Green Garden Design; 82 left GAP Photos / Geoff Kidd; 82 centre GAP Photos / Sabina Ruber; 82 right Photography: Ian Green; 83 left GAP Photos / Clive Nichols; 83 centre GAP Photos / Martin Hughes-Jones; 83 right Photography: Ian Green; 84 Marion Brenner; 85 Claire Takacs; 86–89 Marion Brenner; 90 left M Nevin Smith; 90 centre GAP Photos / Ron Evans; 90 right Ken Gilliland; 91 left GAP Photos / Dave Zubraski; 91 centre Copyright Keir Morse – keiriosity.com; 91 right GAP Photos / Gerald Majumdar; 92 GAP Photos / Jerry Harpur; 93 Photograph Andrew Lawson; 94–97 Harpur Garden Images / Jerry Harpur / Design: Penelope Hobhouse; 98 left GAP Photos / Neil Holmes; 98 centre GAP Photos / Carole Drake; 98 right GAP Photos / J S Sira; 99 left GAP Photos / Martin Hughes-Jones; 99 centre GAP Photos / Andrea Jones; 99 right GAP Photos / J S Sira; 100–101 Raymond Jungles, Inc; 102–105 Lanny Provo; 106–107 Harpur Garden Images / Jerry Harpur / Design: Raymond Jungles; 108 Raymond Jungles, Inc; 109 left & centre Raymond Jungles, Inc; 109 right Fotolia / Michael Roush; 110 Harpur Garden Images / Jerry Harpur / Design: Robert Broekema, Netherlands; 111 Jantiene T Klein Roseboom; 112–113 Harpur Garden Images / Jerry Harpur / Design: Robert Broekema, Netherlands; 114 left GAP Photos / FhF Greenmedia; 114 centre GAP Photos / Mark Bolton; 114 right The Garden Collection / Andrew Lawson; 115 left GAP Photos / Elke Borkowski; 115 centre GAP Photos / Clive Nichols; 115 right GAP Photos / Clive Nichols; 116 Photograph Andrew Lawson / Designer Arabella Lennox-Boyd; 117 Arabella Lennox-Boyd; 118–119 Photograph Andrew Lawson / Designer Arabella Lennox-Boyd; 120 Arabella Lennox-Boyd; 121 Photograph Andrew Lawson / Designer Arabella Lennox-Boyd / Mosaic Designer Maggy Howarth; 122–123 Arabella Lennox-Boyd; 124 left GAP Photos / J S Sira; 124 centre GAP Photos / Martin Hughes-Jones; 124 right GAP Photos / Jerry Harpur; 125 left GAP Photos / Jo Whitworth; 125 centre GAP Photos / Neil Holmes; 125 right GAP Photos / Rob Whitworth; 126 Photograph Andrew Lawson / The Stone House, Wyck Rissington. Designer: Katie Lukas Pond; 127 Photograph Andrew Lawson / The Stone House, Wyck Rissington. Designer: Katie Lukas; 128–129 Photograph Andrew Lawson / The Stone House, Wyck Rissington. Designer: Katie Lukas Waterside planting; 130 left GAP Photos / J S Sira; 130 centre GAP Photos / Elke Borkowski; 130 right GAP Photos / Friedrich Strauss; 131 left GAP Photos / Marcus Harpur; 131 centre GAP Photos / Mark Bolton; 131 right GAP Photos / Jonathan Buckley; 132 GAP Photos / Jerry Harpur / Design: Ulf Nordfjell; 133 Andrea Jones / Garden Exposures Photo Library / Design: Ulf Nordfjell; 134–135 GAP Photos / Jerry Harpur / Design: Ulf Nordfjell; 135 GAP Photos / Jerry Harpur / Design: Ulf Nordfjell; 136–137 GAP Photos / Jerry Harpur / Design: Ulf Nordfjell; 138 left GAP Photos / Fiona Lea; 138 centre GAP Photos / Dave Zubraski; 138 right GAP Photos / Martin Hughes-Jones; 139 left GAP Photos / Andrea Jones; 139 centre GAP Photos / Dave Zubraski; 139 right GAP Photos / Gerald Majumdar; 140 Marion Nickig; 141 Christine Orel; 142–143 Christine Orel; 144 left GAP Photos / Victoria Firmston; 144 centre Christine Orel; 144 right GAP Photos / Rob Whitworth; 145 left GAP Photos / S&O; 145 centre GAP Photos / Martin Hughes-Jones; 145 right Christine Orel; 146 Andrea Jones / Garden Exposures Photo Library / Design: Piet Oudolf; 147 Photograph Andrew Lawson / Design: Piet Oudolf, Hummelo; 148–153 Andrea Jones / Garden Exposures Photo Library / Design: Piet Oudolf; 154 left GAP Photos / Carole Drake; 154 centre GAP Photos / Visions; 154 right GAP Photos / Dianna Jazwinski; 155 left GAP Photos / Julie Dansereau; 155 centre GAP Photos / FhF Greenmedia; 155 right GAP Photos / Jo Whitworth; 156 Photolibrary / Marijke Heuff / Designer: Mien Ruys; 157–159 Tuinen Mien Ruys; 160–161 Photolibrary / Cora Niele / Designer: Mien Ruys; 162 left Andrea Jones / Garden Exposures Photo Library; 162 centre GAP Photos / Pernilla Bergdahl; 162 right GAP Photos / John Glover; 163 left GAP Photos / Martin Hughes-Jones; 163 centre GAP Photos / Richard Bloom; 163 right Photolibrary / François De Heel; 164 Springer Ogden Images; 165 Mark Nowacki; 166–171 Springer Ogden Images; 172 left & centre Springer Ogden Images; 172 right GAP Photos / Christina Bollen; 173 left GAP Photos / Visions; 173 centre & right Springer Ogden Images; 174 MMGI / Marianne Majerus / Design: Tom Stuart-Smith; 175 MMGI / Marianne Majerus; 176–181 MMGI / Marianne Majerus / Design: Tom Stuart-Smith; 182 left GAP Photos / Andrea Jones; 182 centre GAP Photos / Mark Bolton; 182 right GAP Photos / Geoff Kidd; 183 left GAP Photos / Christina Bollen; 183 centre GAP Photos / John Glover; 183 right Gap Photos / Dianna Jazwinski; 184–189 MMGI / Marianne Majerus / Design: Joe Swift; 190 left GAP Photos / Neil Holmes; 190 centre The Garden Collection / Andrew Lawson; 190 right GAP Photos / Geoff Kidd; 191 left GAP Photos / Pernilla Bergdahl; 191 centre GAP Photos / Jonathan Buckley; 191 right GAP Photos / John Glover; 192 Leontine Trijber; 193 GAP Photos / Hanneke Reijbroek; 194 GAP Photos / Jerry Harpur; 195 Leontine Trijber; 196–197 GAP Photos / Jerry Harpur; 198 left GAP Photos / Elke Borkowski; 198 centre GAP Photos / Neil Holmes; 198 right GAP Photos / Victoria Firmston; 199 left GAP Photos / Martin Hughes-Jones; 199 centre & right GAP Photos / Visions; 200 GAP Photos / Jerry Harpur; 201 Andrea Jones / Garden Exposures Photo Library; 202–203 GAP Photos / Jerry Harpur; 204-205 GAP Photos / Nicola Browne; 206 left GAP Photos / Andrea Jones; 206 centre Derek Anderson / Wisconsin Plants http://wisplants.uwsp.edu; 206 right GAP Photos / Dianna Jazwinski; 207 left Wolfgang Oehme, Oehme, van Sweden & Associates; 207 centre GAP Photos / Dianna Jazwinski; 207 right GAP Photos / Richard Bloom; 208–212 Derek St Romaine Garden Photo Library; 213 Cleve West; 214 left GAP Photos / Frederic Didilion; 214 centre GAP Photos / John Glover; 214 right GAP Photos / Martin Hughes-Jones; 215 left GAP Photos / Clive Nichols; 215 centre GAP Photos / Richard Bloom; 215 right GAP Photos / Martin Hughes-Jones

First published in the United Kingdom in 2011 by
PAVILION BOOKS
10 Southcombe Street
London W14 0RA

An imprint of Anova Books Company Ltd

Associate Publisher: Anna Cheifetz
Senior Editor: Emily Preece-Morrison
Designer: Ruth Hope
Picture Researcher: Jenny Faithfull
Copy Editor: Nina Sharman
Proofreader: Caroline Curtis
Indexer: Patricia Hymans

ISBN: 978-1-86205-842-2

A CIP catalogue record for this book is available from the British Library.

10 9 8 7 6 5 4 3 2 1

Reproduction by Rival Colour Ltd., UK
Printed and bound by 1010 Printing International Ltd., China

www.anovabooks.com